DOING THE CONTINENTAL

Advance Praise for *Doing the Continental*

"*Doing the Continental* is very good, wise on all fronts. The chapter on our lack of an energy policy is very convincing."
— Lawrence Martin, columnist and former Washington Bureau chief with the *Globe and Mail*

"Dyment's book provides a provocative assessment of where Canada goes from here in the development of its relationship with the United States. For Dyment, the new 'continental dance' should result in Canada being a more assertive and sophisticated partner.... His book will generate a much-needed debate on Canada's future policy priorities toward the superpower to its south."
— Earl Fry, Ph.D., endowed professor with the David M. Kennedy Center for International Studies of Brigham Young University and past president of the Association for Canadian Studies in the United States

"*Doing the Continental* is timely, well written, and accessible to a broad audience. It covers the major issues in Canada-U.S. relations today and provides a valuable historical perspective. The book's pragmatism and realism make it of value to policy makers."
— Eugene Lang, co-author of *The Unexpected War: Canada in Kandahar*

"In this refreshingly accessible book, David Dyment argues that Canadian discussions of Canada-U.S. relations are so heavily dominated by extreme views that they frequently do more harm than good. His purpose, therefore, is to bring a more balanced perspective to bear. Some may disagree with his positions on specific issues, but much can be learned from the calm display of reason and sanity that he applies to a subject that so often generates more heat than light. His analysis deserves a very wide readership among those interested in Canadian politics and foreign policy."
— Denis Stairs, Ph.D., professor emeritus of political science at Dalhousie University, Fellow of the Royal Society of Canada, and past president of the Canadian Political Science Association

DOING THE CONTINENTAL

A New Canadian-American Relationship

David Dyment

Foreword by Bob Rae

DUNDURN PRESS
TORONTO

Project Editor: Michael Carroll
Editor: Jennifer McKnight
Design: Courtney Horner
Printer: Webcom

Library and Archives Canada Cataloguing in Publication

Dyment, David
     Doing the continental : a new Canadian-American relationship / by David Dyment ; foreword by Bob Rae.

Includes bibliographical references and index.
Issued also in electronic format.
ISBN 978-1-55488-758-3

     1. Canada–Foreign relations–United States. 2. United States–Foreign relations–Canada. 3. Canada–Politics and government–2006-. I. Title.

FC249.D93 2010   327.71073   C2010-902397-8

1   2   3   4   5   14   13   12   11   10

  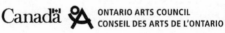

We acknowledge the support of the **Canada Council for the Arts** and the **Ontario Arts Council** for our publishing program. We also acknowledge the financial support of the **Government of Canada** through the **Canada Book Fund** and **The Association for the Export of Canadian Books**, and the **Government of Ontario** through the **Ontario Book Publishers Tax Credit program**, and the **Ontario Media Development Corporation**.

Care has been taken to trace the ownership of copyright materials used in this book. The author and the publisher welcome any information enabling them to rectify any references or credits in subsequent editions.

J. Kirk Howard, President

Published by The Dundurn Group

www.dundurn.com

Dundurn Press	Gazelle Book Services Limited	Dundurn Press
3 Church Street, Suite 500	White Cross Mills	2250 Military Road
Toronto, Ontario, Canada	High Town, Lancaster, England	Tonawanda, NY
M5E 1M2	LA1 4XS	U.S.A. 14150

To Jane, Oliver, and Claire

Contents

Foreword by Bob Rae   9
Preface   11

Part I: Introduction   13
  1 Same Piece of Real Estate?   15
  2 Avro Arrow: The World's Fastest Fighter Jet Runs   19
      Out of Fuel

Part II: Continental Dance: Managing the Relationship   27
  3 Basic Steps   29
  4 Engaging a Preoccupied Partner   35
      Our Segmented Neighbour   40
      The Prime Minister and the President   43
  5 Canada Is Not a Mouse!   47
  6 Big Steps   52
      A Security and Prosperity Partnership?   52
      Was Free Trade Free?   57
  7 Rules for the Dance   63

Part III: Dance Venues   69
  8 What's Mexico Got to Do with It: Continental   71
      Counterweight or Deadweight?
  9 An Energy Superpower Without an Energy Strategy   76
 10 Not Watertight   87
 11 Defrosting Arctic Sovereignty   97

12 Manifest Destiny and Quebec   105

Part IV: Conclusion   115
   13 Beyond Our Shared Continent: Canada in the World   117
      China Card   120
      Iraq, Ballistic Missile Defence, and Afghanistan   120
   14 In the Groove: From Fear to Opportunity   123
      Colonial Mentality   126
      Big Steps, No Thank You   130
      Two Essential Steps   133
      Final Refrain   135

Appendix: Twelve Steps for Doing the Continental   137
Further Reading   139
Acknowledgements   145
Notes   148
Index   163

Foreword
By Bob Rae

Important symbols of Canadian parliamentary sovereignty have been in the custody of the United States for nearly two hundred years, captured by American forces in 1813 when the town of York (now Toronto) was burned and the legislative assembly of Upper Canada was plundered.

In other countries this would have become the subject of intense nationalist feeling and struggle. This has not been so in Canada. Most Canadians and Americans neither know nor care about it. We have grown together on both sides of a remarkably open border, and with the signing of the free trade agreements complete continental integration seemed well underway.

David Dyment explores the deeper dimensions of this relationship, which is not at all simple and has real issues attached to it. The divides have never been unbridgeable, but they are very real, and David's careful scholarship shows how both the federal and provincial governments have wrestled with them in recent years.

These divides include the sheer difference in size and the fact that the border often seems more like a two-way mirror. Because we are so close, Canadians suffer from the illusion that we know the Americans as well as they do themselves. The American illusion is different: they believe that we are "just like them." No doubt John F. Kennedy was right when he said that history and geography made us friends as well as neighbours, but Canada's particular personality and interests do not always converge with our American cousins.

I am always reminded of the simple fact that the majority of U.S. senators come from states with less than 20 percent of the U.S. population: hence our deep trade challenges in softwood lumber, agriculture, and resources. American "exceptionalism" is deeply ingrained in its soul. Canada has no choice but to see itself as an inextricable part of the world itself. We are in the world and the world is in us.

David Dyment explores the dimensions of this unavoidable relationship with intelligence and gusto. His book will help us both to understand each other better.

Preface

President Barack Obama sits down at his desk in the Oval Office for the first time. One of the furthest things from his mind is Canada. From time to time he will receive a briefing that has to do with our country, occasionally a phone call.

On Capitol Hill, the whirling pursuit of interests is intense. The powerful Congress will make decisions based largely on domestic considerations, over which Obama can do little, and which are sometimes not helpful to Canada.

In Ottawa our senior officials worry. "We'll pay a price," they say, for "getting offside" with the Americans. They are too referential to an imperial centre to appreciate that our neighbours aren't even paying attention.

I started this project worried that we were being drawn by the Americans into their maw but soon realized it's not about them, it's about us. It's about how we see ourselves.

As an author, professor, media commentator, Ph.D. in Canadian politics and international relations, and former senior adviser at Foreign Affairs, this was my personal and professional journey to explore Canada's future with the U.S. I travelled with transborder truckers and interviewed ambassadors. I attended a myriad of conferences where advocates from the right and left railed for and against closer relations with the Americans. While I started on the left I soon realized that both the left and the right are waging an ideological, polarized war that has us missing opportunities.

I challenge our continentalist *and* nationalist elites to understand our weaknesses and strengths, our fear of and longing for the U.S., and to lift up Canada's needs rather than laying down ideological creeds. We need to pursue our interests not our ideologies and be aware that the U.S. is a force of nature to be cautiously tamed for our benefit.

Canada's relations with the U.S. are broad and deep, and with Obama in the White House it is a time of hope and renewal. There is a desperate need to gather disparate expertise into a coherent whole. From water to ballistic missile defence, from energy to Arctic sovereignty, my aim is to provide astute, pithy analysis and a crucial new paradigm for our continental dance with our neighbour and for seizing the opportunity to advance Canada's interests.

Part I
Introduction

1

Same Piece of Real Estate?

"You're American."

"No, I'm Canadian."

"Same piece of real estate," he replied.

I didn't know what to say. On the face of it, I couldn't argue with him. I felt frustrated. I wondered what his comment meant, its significance. What are the ramifications of being the "same piece of real estate"? I want to know what to say, to finally be able to respond to Bruce Goff's thought-provoking and irritating comment. A central part of Canada's past, present, and future are informed by his simple observation.

My adventure was tame, not one of desperate third-world poverty and exotic diseases. I was setting out to explore the gentler, Pacific parts of the British Commonwealth. Places mostly like where I'd come from — yet not the United States.

On my first day in New Zealand, I set out to find a *Globe and Mail*. I imagined my search would be aided if I gravitated towards the university. I asked someone where I might find this important link to my recently departed home. As we talked, I learned she was a Labour Party activist deeply involved in a by-election. An election campaign can never have enough workers, and part of an activist's job is to spread the word. I thought of myself as a left-Liberal, and without hesitation I was knocking on doors, singing the praises and policies of a candidate unknown to me.

I found work in Auckland on road crews, on building projects, and as a waiter in a declining luxury restaurant. All the while I continued my involvement with my new political party. That's the context, more than twenty-five years ago, in which I had the epiphany of Goff's comment that helped launch this book. I was at a local party talking to the rather gruff Goff, whose son, still a friend, is currently the leader of the opposition in New Zealand's parliament.

When I left to explore the world, my upbringing had been limited to southwestern Ontario. One of my goals was to understand where I'd come from.

Our relationship with the United States has always fascinated me. From Canada, my father directed a handful of Canadian branch plants in the U.S. Some of my mother's best friends were Americans, their husbands working for U.S. branch plants in Canada. My uncle and great-uncle both left small-town Canada to do what seemed like big things in the U.S. The latter went to work on the Manhattan Project, building the first nuclear bomb, and never returned. My uncle did an M.B.A. at Harvard.

When I came home from school in grade eight, we watched constant coverage of the Watergate hearings. What was I a part of? I knew others, like the Group of Seven, turned to the North and urged us to find meaning in a landscape that would help forge a new Canadian identity.

In my search for Canada, I learned French in my twenties and did a Ph.D. at the Université de Montréal. I wanted to live in what had once been the distant abstraction of Quebec, and understand how to be a Canadian with fellow citizens — people like the francophones in Quebec.

This book is part of that search, an attempt to understand the relationship with our all-so-powerful neighbour. When I was growing up, the U.S. had much more to do with my identity than Quebec, part of my country. The Americans are so much a part of our reality that they contextualize us.

We are coming more fully into the orbit of the U.S. Free trade has hastened this alignment. As a result of the terrorist attacks on the leading symbols of American power, our military, security, and immigration and refugee policies have come to resemble more closely those of our neighbour.

While the arrival of President Obama heralds new opportunities, discussion in Canada of our relations with the U.S. are still mired within a paradigm polarized between rejecting or embracing the Americans. If you think their system and values are superior to ours, the news is good. If the U.S. is anathema to everything you believe in, the trend is bad. But conceptualizing the issue as an ideological battle between patriots and traitors is not a sound basis for understanding.

We must assess our strengths realistically and pursue our interests, aware that the U.S. is not out to destroy us, but is simply a force of nature we must tame for our benefit.

As former Canadian Ambassador to Washington Raymond Chrétien has said:

> The big challenge is how we keep reaping the benefits of our economic integration with the U.S., and use the wealth, the economic power to promote and strengthen our own values, our own beliefs, our own institutions.[1]

And to meet this challenge we need, as former Minister of Foreign Affairs Lloyd Axworthy writes, a new approach:

> One is [labelled either] pro- or anti-American, a nationalist or a continentalist, a free trader or a protectionist. Such stereotyping replaces analysis and obscures the search for thinking and positioning that doesn't fall into either camp.[2]

Doing the Continental leaves the two "stereotypes" described by Axworthy and meets the "challenge" portrayed by Chrétien. It is a call to lay down ideological creeds and lift up Canada's needs.

Far from a middle-of-the-road justification for inaction, the orientation and preoccupations of this book are the basis for taking steps for a more graceful dance with the U.S.

The topic of Canada's relations with the U.S. is big and broad, with experts who advance knowledge by taking manageable objects of study and exploring them in depth. However, this method of exploration is also a weakness — and that weakness is a rationale for this book. There is a need to bring together what is important in considering Canada's future with the United States, to gather up the breaking down of knowledge, to bring it into a coherent whole.

From managing water resources to ballistic missile defence, from energy to Arctic sovereignty, I propose a new paradigm for living with our neighbour that advances our interests.

2

Avro Arrow: the World's Fastest Fighter Jet Runs Out of Fuel

> Ships Hunt for Avro Arrow. Armed with high-tech
> scanners and specially trained divers, two Canadian
> warships probe the depths of Lake Ontario for the
> wreckage of a lost Canadian dream.
>
> June 25, 2004, *Globe and Mail*.

What, exactly, was that Canadian dream? Why is the abrupt way
in which it was cancelled so poignant? What can we learn from
the Arrow about who we are and our national psyche? What does
it tell us about how to advance our interests with the U.S.?

Built to shoot down Soviet bombers coming over the polar
ice cap, the state-of-the-art Arrow flew at twice the speed of sound
and as high as fifty thousand feet. The descendant of the Avro
Canuck, the first jet fighter designed and built in Canada, the
Arrow had thirty-eight thousand parts and drew on the resources
of 654 subcontracting companies.

Prior to the Arrow, Avro produced almost eight hundred
Canucks that were in service throughout the 1950s. With the
success of the Canuck it was logical for Avro to work on a next-
generation aircraft. The company, based outside of Toronto,
had also built one of the world's first commercial jet aircrafts
– the Avro Jetliner, which, while technically sound, was not a
commercial success.

Canada emerged from the Second World War with the
fourth largest economy and military – after the U.S., the

U.K., and France. We were living what many call the Golden Age of Canadian diplomacy. Winston Churchill had given his prescient speech in which he warned that an Iron Curtain had descended in the middle of Europe. An arms race had emerged between two economic and social systems locked in a contest that could lead to nuclear annihilation. Part of that nightmare struggle involved Soviet bombers coming over Canada. Rather than relying on the Americans, we decided to develop a fighter interceptor to stop them ourselves.

The Avro jet fighter, which flew for the first time in March 1958, was based on the British Vulcan bomber with an arrow-like delta wing. Arrow's rationale was to attack bombers, but as the plane came into production it became clear that intercontinental ballistic missiles were a new threat for which the Arrow was not a response.

For the plane to be affordable, Avro would have to sell hundreds to other countries. But the Americans, French, and British all had their own aircraft industries to support and advance.

For largely business reasons, Avro wanted to build all of the systems as well as the engines, fire control, and weapons systems. Then, to reduce the cost of development the decision was made to purchase the fire control and missile system. Still the plane was so expensive it would absorb the entire Canadian defence budget, leaving no money for the navy and army. Would Canada have wanted to continue with the Arrow knowing it meant increasing taxes to expand military spending and slowing the emergence of new social programs, while fuelling a global arms race?

When I set out to examine the story of the Avro Arrow, I was of the view — as so many of us still are — that the aircraft spoke to the promise of our country, and the cancellation to the frustration of that promise. It is also widely believed that the United States was decisive in thwarting our potential. As it turns out, the U.S. was not "the," or even "a," villain.

Indeed, the U.S. was benign in the sense that it did not actively set out to kill the Arrow. The arrival of the missile age did mean the Americans encouraged us to buy its Bomarc missiles, but surface-to-air missiles did not preclude the need for fighter jets. Nevertheless, the U.S. decided not to order any Arrows. It had its own fighter jet manufacturers to support and cannot be blamed for wanting to support and advance its own leading-edge industries.

The United States emerged from the Second World War with 40 percent of the world's economic capacity and in a geopolitical struggle for influence with the Soviet Union. In this context the Americans massively supported the economies of their NATO allies. They made various offers to support the Arrow, short of purchasing it for their own air force. They even offered to help finance building the plane for use by the Royal Canadian Air Force. This was a generous offer, given their self-interest in selling us fighter jets off American assembly lines. Some reports even have the U.S. secretary of the air force saying to the Canadian ambassador, "We'll buy the Arrow and give it to you."[1]

Yet we rejected American assistance as unwanted charity, and a huge chunk of an invaluable industry was lost.

There's no doubt that the Arrow became too expensive for Canada alone to support. Even C.D. Howe — the Liberal minister of everything who, before the Tories took power, had backed Avro and put his protege, Crawford Gordon, in charge of it — said in January 1959, one month before the cancellation, that costs were completely out of hand and that the Arrow should be scrapped.

When the end came in late February 1959, it was haphazard and brutal. In a sense the Arrow had been suffering a slow and steady demise. First the Canadian government was going to buy seven hundred. Then one hundred, and finally it gave the order to destroy thirty-seven of the aircraft — five flown and thirty-two in production.

The death of the Arrow cost nearly twenty-five thousand jobs: fourteen thousand people worked directly on the plane and eleven thousand in support industries. Among the casualties were fifteen hundred highly prized engineers, most of whom were snapped up by leading projects in other countries. Some ended up developing the supersonic Concorde passenger jet. Most went to American aircraft producers or to NASA.

In 1994, during my honeymoon in Louisiana, we stayed at a bed and breakfast where I noticed a model of the Avro Arrow on the mantel. I was shocked to see such a familiar Canadian touch-stone deep in what seemed the strange and different American Deep South. The owner explained that she had grown up as part of "the Avro Arrow family." She said, "I'm bitter Canadians never realized what they threw away, such potential so foolishly discarded." Her father was one of the Avro engineers that went on to help develop the Gemini and Apollo projects.

Perhaps if the Arrow had been less ambitious, less of an all-or-nothing undertaking, it could have more easily survived. At one point, Avro was going to build every aspect of the plane from airframe to engine to weapon and fire control systems. The great strength of the plane, where it truly surpassed others, was its airframe. Why the drive to develop so many other areas of expertise?

One of the reasons is that the Avro and its head, Crawford Gordon, were deeply steeped in Liberal politics, and the new Conservative prime minister, John Diefenbaker, had just defeated the Liberals, his bitter rivals. The way the Arrow was cancelled is tied up with this clash of strong men; it is the background to the curt announcement from the government, followed by the equally abrupt laying off of the Avro workers, a move aimed as a power play to force the government to reconsider. Instead, Diefenbaker ordered all the planes, plans, and data destroyed. Thus, much of the evidence of the greatest achievement in Canadian aviation was eliminated. An additional explanation is that if other countries took an interest in the plane after it was cancelled, but not destroyed, the government would have looked foolish.

Instead, Canada bought sixty-four used Voodoo jet fighters from the U.S. that were barely capable of breaking the sound barrier. The purchase price was $260 million or about $4 million a plane. While some say we could have bought 130 Arrows for that price, that is mythology. The cost per Arrow had climbed to $12 million, or twenty-one Arrows for the same price as the sixty-four Voodoos.

Over time, the Arrow has become a powerful symbol of Canadian prowess, of Canadian leadership, of a path not taken. It is easy to understand the symbolic power of a fighter jet. It is a projection of national force and requires a sophisticated infrastructure to produce, or significant wealth to be able to purchase.

For Canada to design, develop, and build perhaps the leading fighter jet of the era meant, and means, we were succeeding as a very sovereign nation. In building a fighter jet, Canada was making a statement — we can compete with the Americans. We can go into the world without always being contextualized by our relationship to the Americans and their power.

Part of the Arrow mythology is that the plane was the world's most advanced jet-fighter interceptor. Even today, many decades later, the most sophisticated plane in the Canadian Forces — the American-built CF-18 — falls short of some performance levels anticipated of the Arrow had it gone into production.

So how good was the Arrow really? It was an elegant plane, but perhaps not superior. Other planes also almost reached Mach 2 and flew just as high in 1958. How has this fine but not extraordinary airplane taken on such mythic proportions? Canada is not a principal power, nor do we aspire to become one. So why so much angst about the demise of the Arrow?

A lot of the torment has to do with the way it was ended. It would have been better if we could have worked with partners to develop and sell the plane. That might have occurred if we had been more practical, if we had seen the strengths of the plane clearly without the distorting effects of national pride and issues of sovereignty. Instead, we allowed internal partisan struggles to contribute to fuzzy decision making. In the process, we have created a potent and powerful myth that tells us more about ourselves than it does about the airplane.

The fact that Canadians have this strong response to the Arrow tells us we want to be an independent force in the world. We want to develop the infrastructure and technologies to support leading industries. We want to be able to say to ourselves, "We can do it." And we can, but we have to be smart about it. We have to recognize that our tight collaboration with the Americans is an association we can use to advance ourselves, although it also threatens to smoother us. We must always find the path that allows us to do the former without succumbing to the latter. To travel this critical route, we must not fall victim to the dangers of a false debate between rejecting and embracing the United States.

We turned down American assistance for the Arrow as unwanted charity. Yet, we had got ourselves into a project that was beyond our national means. We made a choice that lost us tens of thousands of jobs, cutting-edge technology, and an immense pool of talent that other countries — mostly the U.S. — put to use.

We must learn to work *with* America, understand the reality of our situation, and recognize that its pull — continentalism — is a force of nature. To survive, Canada must harness, temper, control, discipline, and manage this relationship in our interest — not fecklessly succumb to it.

It's not a case of "if you can't beat them, join them." That's a cliché that contributes to foolish, unhelpful, polarized debate. We neither should want to beat them nor join them, but rather work with them to advance what we define as our interests.

We've got to stop characterizing the U.S., a huge and powerful country, as a villain. Such a conceptualization confounds our ability to figure out who we are and how we sensibly fit into North America and the world. It also confuses our thinking both about what makes sense for us and about what we want.

The Arrow points out a tension between our pride and our capacity. Let's get it right from now on. The Arrow shows how we got it dramatically wrong.

Part of why the Arrow sticks in our craw is that for one poignant moment we had the ability to be top gun, to be better than our omnipresent and dominant neighbours.

One of the most memorable moments in the made-for-TV CBC movie, *The Arrow*, comes when the test pilot says to his passenger: "Let's go and wake up the Yanks over at Niagara Air Force base." As they shoot past the base, an American in the control tower says: "What the hell was that?" Well "that" for us was the fleeting pleasure of doing something better than the Americans, and doing it first. And "that" has nothing to do with being anti-American. It's simply about being Canadian and being proud of it. A pro-Canadian moment does not have to be an anti-American one.

Part II
**Continental Dance:
Managing the Relationship**

3
Basic Steps

There is no big solution in our dealings with the United States. Rather, we need to take basic steps and adopt fundamental principles to guide and manage the relationship. To do this we must appreciate how the U.S. system of government works, and how the relationship with our neighbour functions so that we make decisions based on our interests and not our fears, emotions, feelings, ideologies, and old habits of thinking.

Our discussion about the U.S. relationship is senselessly polarized. Our debate amounts to left-nationalists saying integration is bad, stop it, and right-continentalists saying it's good, bring it on. It is time for a change, an opportunity for a more constructive debate.

The U.S. is our best friend, whether we like it or not. It cannot be avoided or dispensed with and it's not a kind of enemy. The real issue is what our interests are. We can't avoid the U.S., yet we have to be mindful that one does not integrate *with* the U.S. but *into* the U.S. Ours is a relationship of two nations, and of the interdependence of two economies. By necessity our friendship with the U.S. needs to be a wary one, as we are a separate country benignly under siege. As a culture, English Canada is somewhat fragile — it's the only OECD country that doesn't have a home-grown drama among its ten most popular TV programs.[1]

We must not be shy about giving our government a mandate to advance our interests. We are a medium-sized country bordering the world's hegemonic power. Our leading industries have been dropping like flies to American and other companies. It makes sense to give our foreign investment review authorities a mandate to consider whether some of these sales are perhaps not in our interest. The Americans, despite their very public adherence to the free market, do not hesitate to disallow and otherwise discourage the sale of American companies when they feel it is not in their national interest.

The credo upon the launching of the CBC is one for Canadians to remember: "The State or the United States." I'm not arguing for or against left or right ideology, I'm simply saying we have a government and in our situation with the U.S. we need to use it.

When we mindlessly reject things as American, we are doing ourselves a disservice. We can't have a rational debate about health care because it is shut down by the phrase "American-style health care." Don't get me wrong, I don't want a system of health care that wastes billions of dollars on unnecessary administration and leaves millions uninsured. But I do think we would be well served by a reasonable debate. Right now we can't benchmark our health care system against ones in France, Germany, Scandinavia, and the U.K. because some elements of these are described as "American-style." It is a weakness for Canada to be caught in this polarized anti-America–pro-America dichotomy. It's hard for Canada to win when our debate is ill-framed.

We need to outgrow our habit of fighting for or against an imperial connection, first with the British and now the Americans. It is an old way of thinking, and a paradigm that allows us to miss what makes sense for Canada. The question that needs to be foremost in our mind is "What makes Canada as strong as possible?"

We must creatively mix points of view to arrive at policy prescriptions that respond to our needs, not to our ideologies. We let ideology interfere with what makes sense for Canada.

Canada objectively has interests: let's advance them. We must take the best of the nationalist school, its counsel of caution in our relations with the U.S., and the best of the integrationist school in its appreciation that some of our national interests are served by our relations with the U.S.

As I've said, I've done some of the research for this book by going to what seems like every conference on the subject. I can tell you it is very different going to a lefty conference than to a right-wing conference on this issue. The former is full of serious indignation and the latter serious purpose. At a right-wing conference American speakers are, if not stars, important and listened to carefully.

At a lefty conference, the American speaker has to pass a litmus test. They have, after all, been invited so they've generally passed this, and within about three minutes also pass the test with the general audience. They are then treated respectfully, and always with a large dose of consideration that the guest has also solicited — consideration that it's difficult being an American progressive activist and particularly one who painfully and bravely persists in living in the United States.

From the coal face of our polarized discussion about our future with the U.S., I always come away thinking that somewhere between these divergent mindsets there must be a third way.

The left and right tell us we have a problem. Like with any problem, what's required is a solution. Part of defining and finding a third path is to stop looking for *the* solution. Our relationship with the U.S. is a paradox. It is simultaneously both dangerous and helpful. Understanding this moves us out of, past, and beyond the old paradigm of left and right ideology and imperial connections.

We must dissolve and drive from our minds the old conceptual framework with its comfortable and tired rhetoric, touchstones, and shibboleths so that a new model of understanding can emerge which embraces the contradiction of our relations with the U.S.

There is an enduring paradox to be managed. The new paradigm requires we put at the centre of our understanding the contradiction that the U.S. simultaneously both assists and hinders us. It cannot be avoided or dispensed with. There is no problem to be solved, but rather an enduring situation to be managed. This is why this part of the book about managing our relationship with the U.S. is central to my thesis.

Those who advocate big solutions of a NAFTA-Plus variety seem oblivious that continentalism is a force of nature that should not be encouraged, as it threatens to consume us. Society in the U.S. is more neoconservative than in Canada, more supportive of minimalist government and lower taxes. Within Canada the orientation of leading business organizations, while outside the Canadian mainstream, is within the norm of American opinion. Perhaps this is one of the reasons Thomas d'Aquino, associated with the Canadian Council of Chief Executives, and Nancy Hughes Anthony, formerly with the Canadian Chamber of Commerce, advocate further integration with the U.S. — it is a way of advancing the economic interests of their members and of making Canadian society more like that of the United States.

Advocates from both groups with the best of intentions can inflame Canadians understanding of the U.S., doing us a disservice, whether it is nationalist Linda McQuaig (promoting her recent book *Holding the Bully's Coat*[2]) who spent five minutes of a forty-five-minute talk on American invasion plans for Canada, or d'Aquino telling us "security trumps trade," and our only course is to fall in line with the U.S. Both are respected and influential proponents of the two sides of the debate, as it is currently structured, and both misunderstand our relationship with the U.S. Not only does the current debate have its advocates talking past each other, but their battle has a lack of reality to it. These are the very conditions that signal and precede a paradigm shift.

Ironically, the prescriptions of the left and the right take us to the same outcome! D'Aquino feels it is very logical and normal that in our relationship with the U.S. we will enter into a Customs Union and a Monetary Union. A Customs Union means Canada and the U.S. would have a single uniform tariff for the rest of the world. A Monetary Union means both countries would have one currency.

Maude Barlow would have us avoid the U.S. — costing us jobs, giving our children fewer opportunities, and making us poorer. That route poorly positions us to face the force of the U.S., and would eventually have a dramatic integrative outcome.

Barlow and d'Aquino lead us to the same outcome. D'Aquino's approach gets you a Customs Union and a Monetary Union. Barlow's approach leads to economic decline and less negotiating power, in which the ensuing crisis would still lead to d'Aquino's end point. These diametrically opposed approaches to Canada's relationship with the U.S. take us by different routes to the same end.

We are walking the line of a ridge. To have significantly more or less integration is to tumble down one side or the other. Rhetorically, we are told the "status quo is not an option," when it is largely the only option.

The U.S., a huge presence, is not going away. Our starting point must be to recognize and manage that reality. That must be the premise we start from, which will give us prescriptions and outcomes. From the two false premises, with which we are currently sadly saddled, come poor prescriptions and unnecessary and undesirable outcomes.

This part of the book explores fundamental ideas for understanding the relationship and how to manage it. A central element, and truth, is that we don't understand the United States: how it's society works or how it's system of government works. We imagine the Americans think about us, but they don't. When I asked Colin Robertson, the former head of outreach to Congress at our embassy in Washington, "What do they think about Canada?" he replied, "They don't think about Canada!" Such an attitude should not be disappointing or frustrating; it is an opportunity. It means we have a freedom we haven't allowed ourselves.

With a fresh approach, we can see there are things in our history with the U.S. that could have happened that did not, and things that are now possible. As explored in the previous chapter, we might have made the Avro Arrow a success. And as we will see in future chapters, we would not focus on Mexico and we would look to our energy reserves for our needs and not those of the Americans — and know the difference. We might see the Americans as allies in the Arctic rather than as bullies. We could have said "no" to ballistic missile defence without the hand-wringing. We would not have gone to Afghanistan in the way we have. Canadians there would not have died — and some that may in the future will not have to.

By taking some time to understand how our neighbour works, we are in a much better position to manage relations with them so that we get the most out of it for ourselves — not selfishly or with anti-Americanism, but sensibly.

4
Engaging a Preoccupied Partner

The U.S. is a vast, self-contained world within the world. It spans the most fertile and temperate part of the western hemisphere. With more than 300 million people and the world's richest economy, it's self-absorbed. This combined with a powerful Congress with members being re-elected every two years means it's law makers are excruciatingly sensitive and responsive to the interests of their constituents.

The House of Representatives has 435 seats, and to win the day 218 votes are needed. Much of the decision-making at the federal level in the U.S. comes down, as a senior congressional figure told me, to those 218 votes.

This is important for Canadians to keep in mind. So much of what emanates from Washington has nothing to do with other countries, or with Canada, it has to do 435 members of Congress being re-elected every two years and passing legislation in the House of Representatives. U.S. policy is about domestic interests operating within a remarkably self-contained and self-absorbed world.

This is reinforced by the fact that extraordinarily little of American wealth comes from exports: only about 10 percent. So while about 20 percent of U.S. exports go to Canada, that is less than 2 percent of U.S. gross domestic product!

Other than the world's hot spots into which the U.S. is drawn, the outside world simply doesn't appear upon the mental map of most Americans.

Here's an example: an exact quote as related to me by a Canadian minister who was part of a small dinner with former President George W. Bush in the dining room off the Oval Office. The discussion turned to Devils Lake where water is being diverted from North Dakota into Manitoba. Bush, after much listening, finally said, "You're telling me this water runs into Canada, but water doesn't run south to north."

What Bush meant to say was "In the U.S., water for the most part runs north to south, sometimes to the east and west, but rarely from the south to the north." The head of the United States had seldom been outside of the U.S. before becoming president. Like so many of his fellow citizens he is wonderfully insular and self-absorbed. The U.S. is his world. A world of rivers like the Mississippi and Hudson that run north to south.

Bush resonates so well with average Americans because they see things the same way. For the average American, water doesn't flow south to north. It's not that it can't, it just doesn't.

This is what that vast, self-contained world looks and feels like, with its powerful Congress constantly and highly responsive to domestic interests. This is the world, through growing integration with the U.S., into which Canada is being drawn.

Relations between the two countries are so broad and deep that the current structures of their management do not reflect the reality of the situation. As Canada's economic space is increasingly becoming more integrated with America's, the Canadian political space is infused from the U.S. Therefore, there is a steady pressure to find new ways of engaging and interacting with the United States.

To reflect and better capture what's happening, we are increasingly moving beyond the normal models within which nation states interact, and increasingly organizing some of our systems of government to align with, and engage, the Americans'. The federal government, in both Canada and the U.S., is reorganizing and expanding initiatives to engage the Americans. In the U.S. we are opening more offices: a massive increase of thirteen offices to forty-one. Author and columnist Jeffery Simpson captures the logic:

> The Congress and the administration represent the basket, where points are scored. The whole country is the basketball court, where plays develop and strategies unfold that eventually lead to something happening around the basket. There are no lay-ups or slam dunks or 15-foot jumpers without playing well over the whole court.[1]

In Washington we have set up a new branch in our embassy to focus on Congress. Our embassy representatives visit Congress daily to lobby members and their staffs on how their districts are affected by Canada. Through a new database, they point out how many jobs amongst their constituents are dependent on Canadian employers.

While former Canadian ambassador to Washington, Allan Gotlieb, claims to be the inventor of lobbying Congress, he didn't so much invent it as respond in the mid-1980s to the failure of an east coast fisheries agreement in which two U.S. senators reacted to pressure from a few hundred scallop fisherman and derailed a treaty that had been negotiated and signed by the two governments.

The move to put more gears, and oil, into the U.S. system means we are becoming more a part of that system. Former Prime Minister Paul Martin created a committee on our relations with the U.S. in our federal cabinet. And some, such as former Deputy Prime Minister John Manley and former Alberta Premier Peter Lougheed, are advocating that our ambassador to the U.S. should be a member of cabinet, so, as Manley says, "He would have real clout in D.C."

The launch in March 2005 of the Security and Prosperity Partnership (SPP) was part of this process of striving for closer cooperation. It represents an understanding between the leaders of Canada, the U.S., and Mexico to enhance coordination of their economic and security relations. For Canada's purposes, it is about more fully harmonizing our procedures and regulations with the U.S. The SPP recognizes that three can talk, but two can do. Both Canada and Mexico are largely engaged in separate discussions with the U.S. on many issues. This is consistent with the findings, in a later chapter, about how Mexico should sensibly fit into our relations with the U.S.

These initiatives that involve reorganizing government capacity and procedures — be they special committees of cabinet or the processes of the SPP — are measures of our growing integration. This is a process whose ultimate logic, if we are not mindful of the dangers, is direct Canadian representation in the U.S. Congress.

As we have seen, both sides of the debate over our relations with the U.S. frame it as a problem. Right-continentalists tell us they have a big solution to the problem. A problem with these big solutions is they put us in huge asymmetries of size and power. Take one of their favourite proposals, a monetary union. At best, Canada would become the thirteenth regional Federal Reserve bank, joining the twelve that currently shape U.S. monetary policy.

There is, however, one notable anomaly to this problem of asymmetry: the International Joint Commission (IJC). Formed in 1909, the IJC manages environmental issues along the border. Each country has three commissioners, and all decisions require a majority vote. It's a system for making decisions, which, apparently, the U.S. doesn't like and can't believe it's saddled with; it is not the way the U.S. is used to operating around the world. It exists as a special case, perhaps because it was signed with Great Britain near the height of its power, and because it is about managing a border that is done most effectively jointly. It is understood as a "narrow gauge" organization, not transferable to other areas of the management of our relationship with our neighbour.

What about that biggest of big solutions — formally joining the United States, becoming part of the Union? Surely that is the most decisive way to have influence in Washington.

If part of the premise is that there is a problem to be solved — the biggest of big solutions would not solve the problem either. We would have less power than California. That state, the largest in the union, has a population of over 36 million. It has fifty-three of 435 seats in the House of Representatives. Even with so many seats, California's voice is never decisive. Canada's population of 33 million would give us perhaps forty-eight seats. We would, however, do better than California in Senate seats. That state, like all others, has two seats. Canada could be expected to come to the Union as at least five states — perhaps as British Columbia, the rest of the West, Ontario, Quebec, and the Atlantic. Still, that's only ten Senate seats out of 110. Clearly, formal integration into the Union is not a solution.

With NAFTA we have a dispute settlement mechanism, and now the continentalist right would have us contemplate a NAFTA-Plus to further stabilize our relationship with the U.S. There is an irony that the more deals we do with the U.S., to bring our relationship within special norms, the more we become subject to U.S. practices, to the point that we become a part of U.S. practices.

It's easy to see how this can and, perhaps in the fullness of time, will happen. Here's what then-Maryland Senator Joseph Biden said of Prime Minister Martin after they met in April 2004:

> He got it right away. I could have just as easily been speaking to the president of the U.S., or governor of a state, or one of my colleagues in the U.S. Senate. It didn't need any translation. It's one of those incredible things about the

relationship. You don't have to explain. You sort of finish each other's sentences. Canada and the U.S., it's like ham and eggs. It's kind of hard to separate them whether we like it or not.[2]

"Getting it" is a precursor to "getting together." You've got to wonder if union, despite its shortcomings, isn't in our future.

One can also imagine scenarios where further integration with the U.S. might happen suddenly. This could happen, for example, if there was a simultaneous terrorist attack on Canada and the U.S. Imagine also that the president was more in the mould of John Kerry — from a northern liberal state, played hockey, and spoke French — and saw the role of the U.S. not in unilateralist terms but in a multilateralist sense. Add to this a president who took a personal interest in Canada and was well disposed to Canada and the Canadian prime minister. Like Ronald Regan was toward Brian Mulroney, and who suggested a Canadian attend meetings of the U.S. cabinet. A president who might advance a joint currency when the Canadian dollar was 25 percent lower than the U.S. dollar, yet still propose that the Canadian dollar be merged at par.

The ball, as they say, is very much in our court. It's up to us to decide how involved we want to be in this process of integration. Where is our centre of gravity in our relations with the United States? Will it someday be said, "It started with a Canadian cabinet committee on the U.S., and ended with a Canadian in the U.S. cabinet?"

Our Segmented Neighbour

One of the big mistakes we make in dealing with the U.S., in fact the *biggest* mistake, is that we don't properly understand how the U.S. political system works.

We imagine that because we are exposed to the U.S. every day that we have a pretty good idea of how things work south of the border. That is a conceit that hurts us. The U.S. is a much more regional country than we realize, and the U.S. political system arrives at decisions in a way that is so foreign to our own that we don't get it. As a result we misunderstand the U.S. and make wrong decisions.

In our system, the prime minister has only one political constraint — the ability to get decisions through Parliament — in a majority government that is particularly easy. We think the president and the prime minister can agree on something and that's all that's necessary. It doesn't work that way. As former ambassadors to the U.S. have written, "The players are so numerous and dispersed you can never explain what actually happened," and "If anyone tells you he knows where a particular decision was made in Washington, he is either a fool or a liar."[3]

Once one considers the sheer size and scope of the U.S. and the division of powers between the president, the Congress, and the judiciary, the concept of building political capital in Washington is of limited value. And yet our pundits and politicians — including senior ministers — insist on analyzing and acting on the basis of a false understanding. Perhaps it's because their egos get in the way of appreciating both our country's insignificance and their personal insignificance in how decisions get made in the U.S. capital. Too often senior ministers think that because they have a relationship with their U.S. counterpart that Canada's policy needs to reflect the views of their American interlocutors.

The U.S. is simply not keeping track of whether Canada has been helpful. Our ministers are stroking their egos and making poor decisions for Canada if they allow their judgment to be clouded by misunderstanding how significant they are to their American counterparts. Think of the U.S. president, as an example, who spends not days but only hours each year thinking about Canada.

The U.S. is preoccupied with so many issues that as long as Canada doesn't work actively to counter U.S. interests, we don't register in their thoughts. What Canada does or doesn't do is more irrelevant in the American political system than we realize. We are taken for granted. It's a mistake to think that we need to play a "war-fighting" role in Afghanistan because we didn't go to Iraq. A former chief of staff to our minister of defence says the decision to play our current role in Afghanistan was due to the minister and other government leaders feeling we had to assuage U.S. opinion because we hadn't supported Ballistic Missile Defence (BMD). In fact, the U.S. was going ahead with BMD regardless of what Canada did and wasn't that concerned about the Canadian decision.

Moreover, there is no spillover from such a strictly military issue into U.S. economic policy. A dramatic example of this is the U.S. Congress placing stiff tariffs on U.K. steel despite U.K. participation and leadership in Iraq and Afghanistan. And textiles from Pakistan, a key ally of the U.S. in the fight against terrorism, continue to face prohibitive U.S. tariffs. The U.S. is a vast, self-absorbed, and *segmented* world.

One should not forget the nature of the U.S. bureaucracy in all of this. It is massive and, like Congress, lacks cohesion and reflects divergent and competing views and opinions. So, like Congress, the U.S. bureaucracy is not going to turn as one corporate entity and promote or punish Canada.

This is how Michael Kergin, a former Canadian ambassador to the U.S., put it to me: "Think of at least three kinds of events – political, economic, and military. Three parts of the jungle. The three constituencies are very different. Be skeptical about linkages among them."[4]

The sheer size and power of the U.S., combined with its system of government, leads to decisions that affect other countries. But these decisions do not make the U.S. bad. Not honouring a NAFTA dispute settlement panel ruling does not really make the U.S. bad; it's a reflection of its heft, combined with the nature of its Congressional system of government.

We are not going to change either the sheer power of the U.S. or its Congressional system of government, with the prerogatives of powerful senators and members of the House of Representatives to protect their constituents' jobs and money.

The NAFTA Dispute Settlement Mechanism does not change that, but it does help to condition the outcome of disputes, such as those over softwood lumber. Canada did not get everything it wanted, and was awarded by the dispute settlement mechanism, but in late 2006 it did agree to 80 percent of what it was due, with approximately $1 billion held back from the $5 billion collected in inappropriate penalties.

Interests in our self-absorbed, segmented neighbour often work in alignment with Canadian interests to determine outcomes. On soft wood, part of the pressure in the U.S. to resolve the issue was from the U.S. National Association of Home Builders and from the American soft wood companies that own 40 to 45 percent of the Canadian industry.

The Prime Minister and the President

While we may on occasion want our prime minister to express indignation to the president, there is not a lot the president can do — are we asking him to change the U.S. system of government and decision making? A close associate of Prime Minister Jean Chrétien told me of a meeting he was at in the Oval Office, where former President George W. Bush said to Chrétien: "If you can't convince Senator Baucus from Montana, who is the head of the Commerce Committee, then I'd like to help but there's not much I can do." At best, all the president *can* do is use some of his limited political capital with Congress. And he normally needs all of that to advance his administration's policies. When we ask the president to make the Canadian position part of his policies, how does that help his survival and success which depend on his sway among Americans and American interests, not among Canadians and Canadian interests?

As former Canadian ambassador to the U.S., Michael Kergin says, "The president operates in a free market economy. Congress is supreme in trade policy, the president is making all the time, all kinds of deals with Congress. So how much of his capital is he going to use in an area in which he has little power to help another country?"

The relationship does not at all work on the basis that if you lose favour in the White House you pay a big price. It is better to have good executive to executive relations, but so much of U.S. decision making is associated with Congress.

Speculating on relations between the two leaders is something of a parlour game. Not infrequently, I'm asked by the media to comment on aspects of the Canada-U.S. relationship. Their favourite question is, "How is our prime minister getting along with the president, and what does this mean?"

As you know, here's my answer: "Their relationship is but a part of a broad and deep interaction between the two countries. Moreover, the president doesn't have that much power in our relations with the U.S. He constantly has to consider Congress. And Congress has jurisdiction over a lot of the issues like U.S. trade laws that preoccupy Canadians."

The relationship of our leaders is important because it sets a tone. But it's very rare that a president is willing to use much political capital with Congress to advance an issue brought to him by our prime minister. The president has far too many more pressing and difficult domestic and international issues that he has to arm wrestle with Congress.

There are some examples where the president has intervened. On the management of the acid rain file, Ronald Reagan told his aides to "help his friend Brian." Yet by the time the U.S. moved, the issue had become a big fight in the U.S. and the outcome can be understood in terms of U.S. domestic politics. Another example — as the scholar of Canadian foreign policy, John Holmes, has written — was when Lyndon Johnson used his influence, though not decisive, to advance the auto pact when Lester Pearson had helpfully sent peacekeepers to Cyprus.[5]

The chemistry between the two leaders is affected by numerous factors. One of those is values. How do they see the world and each other's country? Harper and Bush shared a starting point in that they have similar values. Chrétien was more inclined to see the U.S. as selfish and crime ridden and as a source of discord in the world. He even suggested that the U.S., in part, brought the terrorist attacks of 9/11 upon itself.

The chemistry that comes from personal foibles is also important. Chrétien was less comfortable with politicians who started life with privilege. In contrast, Martin and Bush come from a family dynasty. Yet, Chrétien and Bush share a business-like approach to issues, neither of them being policy wonks like Martin and Clinton. Currently, while both policy-oriented, Harper and Obama have different ideological starting points.

In the end, neither Chrétien nor Martin got along terribly well with Bush. But surely this is not so much their fault, as some would suggest. Why should the onus be on our prime minister to get along when it was perhaps Bush's unilateralist approach and lack of diplomatic interpersonal skills that were the problem?

We focus too much upon this level of the relationship. "Building Cross-Border Links: A Compendium of Canada–U.S. Government Collaboration," produced by the Canadian government, contains a list of all the myriad processes and agreements between the two countries.[6] Among them are: forums, task forces, advisory groups, working groups, joint commissions, boards, panels, and meetings of premiers and governors. This supports the reality that there is an unprecedented depth and breadth to the relationship, of which relations between the prime minister and president is only a part. There is a thicket of joint activity that structures the Canada-U.S. relationship from which the prime minister and the president only occasionally stick out their heads.

5

Canada Is Not a Mouse!

One of the great disservices of those who advocate for closer ties with the United States is their view that Canada is preternaturally vulnerable to the U.S., and that we must do everything possible to satisfy the Americans or the consequences will be severe.

This argument fails to appreciate a number of factors. Chief among them is that the U.S. also needs Canada.

In the months after the terrorist attacks on the U.S. in September 2001, leading right-continentalists advanced big solutions in the face of Canadian vulnerability to U.S. security concerns.

There are two fundamental problems with the premise behind these "solutions." First, as we know, our relations with the U.S. require careful management, not solutions. Secondly, the relationship with the U.S. is one of mutual interdependence.

Both countries are highly motivated to maintain the smooth flow of cross-border traffic. Canada is the largest export market for thirty-seven of the fifty U.S. states. Trade with Canada supports over 5.2 million U.S. jobs. On average, a car assembled in the U.S. contains parts that have crossed the border six times. Virtually all the natural gas the U.S. imports is from Canada, and Canada is its largest source of imported oil. All of this trade, from Canada to the U.S., and from the U.S. to Canada, amounts to almost $2 billion a day.

Canada purchases over 20 percent of all U.S. exports. That is more than the U.S. exports to the twenty-seven members of the European Union. More exports from the U.S. flow over the

Detroit-Windsor Ambassador Bridge than all its exports to Japan. Here is how one U.S. government documents puts it:

> Canada is our largest supplier of energy. Our exports to Canada exceed our combined exports to Mexico and Japan, our second and third largest export markets. And Canada plays a key role in the U.S. manufacture of motor vehicles, lumber and metal products.[1]

Our relationship with the U.S. has a momentum of its own based on massive and mutual self-interest. For leading Canadian right-continentalists to confidently state "security trumps trade" and that Canada therefore must fall into line with U.S. policies is simplistic and fanciful. Sadly, it is a rhetoric used to scare Canadians into *not* standing up for ourselves.

Let's look at this phrase "security trumps trade," which sets out to define the terms of debate and seems, on the face of it, to be irrefutable. The Canadian Trucking Association says the impact of current border security regulations reduces trade by $1 billion a year, or the value of just half of one day's trade. So does "security trump trade"? No, half a day of one-year's trade is not security trumping trade. If anything is doing the trumping in this misleading assertion, it's trade trumping security!

At one of the many conferences I attended as research for this book, one leading American analyst said d'Aquino's transcendent identity, and loyalty, is to his class not his country. Another American, a prominent proponent of continental integration, Sidney Weintraub said the U.S. has a "vital interest in keeping the border open, and even an implied threat by the U.S. to do otherwise is madness."

The U.S. is not defensible without close security cooperation from Canada. Canada has lots of cards. Why underplay our hand?

Pierre Trudeau famously said, "Living beside the United States is like a mouse sleeping with an elephant." The observation is half true, but half dangerous.

The true part concerns the random movements and size of an elephant. It's a useful quote so far as it describes the way the U.S. governmental system works. The dangerous, untrue part that sticks in most people's minds is that Canada is a mouse. It's not!

It's a quote that is used to stress our vulnerability to the U.S. The U.S. system also protects Canada. After 9/11, we were told by right-continentalists that the U.S. would advance its interests and move against those of Canada if we did not respond on security issues. Yes, it's true we needed to respond on security issues and we did. But Congress is full of all kinds of border state and transborder business interests that need a continuation of good relations and efficient movement of goods and people across the border.

Closing the border with Canada would trigger thousands of local U.S. issues. U.S. politicians act in response to local issues. All politics, as the saying goes, is local. Here are some examples: when new residency rules were proposed for snowbirds, Florida politicians reversed them; when the number of Ontario students studying in Michigan was to be restricted, Michigan politicians weighed in. Members of Congress were decisive in determining a positive outcome.

Regionally, and sectorally, when the Americans have a problem, their politicians respond. The idea that Canada is a timid and preternaturally vulnerable mouse, and that congruent interests in the U.S. are not engaged, is simplistic and not true.

It is often said that Canada is a country without a region. For example, Australia and New Zealand, less influential countries than Canada, are understood to have a zone of influence, to be regional powers, in the South Pacific. If the premise is that all countries have regions upon which they have influence, Canada is said to leapfrog the U.S. and have influence in the Caribbean. But it is logical, and rarely considered, that Canada has influence on parts of the United States, and that those areas are also part of our region

It is good for us to realize that along our border, and deeper into the U.S. hinterland in different economic sectors, we have influence. We are a power in North America. We are not only acted upon.

In geographic terms, Canada looms large in places like Plattsburgh in upper New York State and in Buffalo. Yukon and British Columbia are a significant presence in Skagway, Alaska. In northern Maine, Canadian economic interests are particularly active, and Manitoba and Ontario are a prominent influence in northern Minnesota. Even if the combined U.S. population of such areas is only two million, that's perhaps more people than there are in Australia's or New Zealand's zones of influence in the South Pacific.

If two million people are at the centre of our regional influence, think of our influence beyond that core. First, our influence extends to the 37 million Americans who live within two hundred miles (320 kilometers) of the Canadian border, an area that includes suburbs of such cities as New York, Chicago, and Seattle. It also extends to the thirteen states with a combined population of 75 million that share a common border with Canada.

For Canada to be a power in such a significant region is an advantage for us, and translates into influence upon their domestic politics. We are a taker, but also a *shaper* of American policy.

All things considered, our relationship with the U.S. is more analogous to an elephant in bed, not with a mouse, but with a smallish hippo, a buffalo, or muskox. The dynamics of the U.S. system of government do not allow it to be oblivious to Canada and, specifically, to cross-border interests.

That's what interdependence is about. The U.S. has an element of dependence upon Canada within its own interests.

Take the just-in-time deliveries of auto parts from Canada that millions of U.S. jobs depend upon. Look at the huge amount of energy the U.S. imports from Canada, like 40 percent of California's supply of natural gas!

U.S. decision making may move erratically like an elephant, but when it comes to Canada, it's not in bed with a mouse! That's something Canadians need to understand, so that we make sound decisions that are in our interest.

6
Big Steps

As has been said, we are prone to the big solution in managing our relationship with the U.S. None has been bigger in recent times than free trade, a key recommendation in 1985 of the Royal Commission on the Economic Union and Development Prospects for Canada, struck three years earlier by Liberal Prime Minister Pierre Trudeau. The Conservatives, lead by Brian Mulroney, were overtaken by scandals from 1984 to 1988, but by holding an election on free trade, they were able to radically change the dynamics of the vote. The Tories were re-elected, and the Canada-U.S. Free Trade Agreement followed. This was later superseded by the North American Free Trade Agreement (NAFTA), which included Mexico.

The terrorist attacks on September 11, 2001, brought something called the September 12 effect — a crisis in the management of goods and people across the border. There were long line-ups as all cars and trucks were searched upon entering the U.S.

This lead to a resounding call from right-continentalists in Canada for another big solution, often described as a NAFTA-Plus of further integration with the U.S.

A Security and Prosperity Partnership?

Jumping to 2007, the August news lull was about to be filled by a cacophony of coverage about the Security and Prosperity

Partnership's (SPP) third annual meeting to be held for the first time in Canada on August 20.

President George W. Bush, Mexico's then-president Vicente Fox, and our Paul Martin launched the SPP in Waco, Texas, in March 2005. It's an attempt to continue the NAFTA process, and provide a structure to deal with security concerns arising from 9/11; hence "security" and "prosperity" in a partnership.

The SPP emerged from an initiative Canada took to the Americans in the weeks after 9/11 — the Smart Border Accord. Much of what the SPP deals with is a continuation of that accord with bureaucratic acronyms like FAST for "Free and Secure Trade Program," which now deals with FAST lanes at border crossings.

At the SPP meeting in Montebello, Quebec, an hour's drive from Ottawa, the leaders announced a joint strategy for dealing with pandemic disease. The partnership, for now, is addressing obvious and bureaucratic measures, and like the Accord it reassures the Americans by turning problems into a partnership.

The SPP has no time frames for realizing goals, and responsibility for achieving targets is not conferred on any organization. It largely consists of existing activities and policies across a number of government departments placed under a single rubric.

Meetings of the SPP by government leaders are about checking in, not big announcements. At the second meeting in Cancun in March 2006, the leaders promised to "coordinate, advise and consult on issues of joint concern," and by 2008 these gatherings were being re-branded as meetings of the North American leaders. While a number of bureaucratic sails are partially on one platform they are not sailing any ships of state.

Why is a routine undertaking causing such a fuss? Well, there are two reasons. One is that it's a slippery slope between a FAST lane and a customs union: both speed things up at the border. How do we draw a line between the mundane and the monumental? The other is that the process is being advised from civil society exclusively and somewhat secretively by business groups with names like the Canadian Council of Chief Executives and the North American Competitiveness Council. These are associated with largely secret meetings that produce documents with phrases — which come to light as a result of access to information requests — like this one: "To what degree does a concept of North America help/hinder solving problems between the three countries? While a vision is appealing working on the infrastructure might yield more benefit and bring more people on board ('evolution by stealth')."[1]

While there is little wind in the SPP's sails, some business leaders have great — and as yet unfulfilled — ambitions for the partnership. After 9/11, there were thirteen proposals in two years from the continentalist right to go beyond NAFTA to take the next step with a big idea, a grand bargain.[2]

Realizing no such deal was emerging, leading continentalists started thinking about creating the necessary preconditions for what they often term a NAFTA-Plus, and began to advance the concept of a North American Community. For them, the SPP is about incremental steps leading to a customs union of common external tariffs and perhaps even a monetary union.

Now that some time has passed, post 9/11 big ideas can be seen as part of the waxing and waning of the continentalist impulse. There is a huge gap between the rhetoric and ambitions of the SPP's business boosters and the reality of the partnership.

What opponents of the SPP are mostly making a fuss about are the privileged access, secret meetings, and grand ambitions of the SPP's business advisers. And with this brush they are tarring the SPP. Together, in an unwitting dance, opponents and proponents are sowing confusion as to just what, at least currently, the SPP is.

It's true that the SPP is an opportunity to retrofit NAFTA, and opponents in Canada — such as the Council of Canadians — are right in flagging a potential danger, even if it is relatively moribund.

For Canada, the SPP, as it is currently manifest, is largely a response to our needs and interests, not our ideologies. To reprise, "The U.S. is our best friend, whether we like it or not." We are in an enduring relationship best subject to careful management, not big solutions.

The SPP, of no dramatic results and lots of controversy, is caught in our familiar polarized right-continentalist/left-nationalist debate with the debaters talking past each other. We are suffering an abdication by our policy-making community of its responsibility — with Tom d'Aquino infusing the SPP with grand objectives and Maude Barlow earnestly sounding the alarm.

The reality is that there is not a generalized appetite for the SPP to be much more than it is today. The bulk of Canadian opinion is skeptical: the U.S. is very protective of its prerogatives and U.S. state legislatures are passing resolutions denouncing it, and in Mexico NAFTA has perhaps been the least successful.

A dramatic departure from the SPP's current format will require a lot of public debate and parliamentary engagement, something that is not on the agenda of politicians in any of the three countries.

The political systems of these countries are far too complex and multifaceted to think that just because their leaders meet that a dramatic outcome must follow. This, as discussed, is particularly true of the U.S. with its rigorous division of responsibilities and powerful Congress.

While the SPP is not insignificant, it is much less than what its boosters want and its detractors fear.

The SPP is a wonderful mobilizing and organizing tool for the left. The leader of the Green Party, Elizabeth May, has said it's the overarching frame for policies. But can it really carry that much freight? Fighting the SPP brings together left-progressive activists within Canada and North America. As discussed by the Canadian Labour Congress, "There has never been a better time for co-coordinated reflection and action between activist communities in North America."[3] This helps to build the concept of a North American Community, which is something ironically also advocated for by right-continentalists who see it as part of the psychological pre-conditions for the realization of their integrationist dreams.

The right and left once again unwittingly come together — in this instance to advance the concept of a North American Community. One sees this also in the academic community where professors from both perspectives are launching Centres for the Study of North America with enrollment encouraged from the three North American countries. This is, in part, made possible by funding from governments and foundations.

While the rhetoric of the left and right can make it a challenge to assess the reality of the SPP, one advantage of the partnership is it reassures Washington that there is a bureaucratic process in place that normalizes the challenges, and is helpful politically.

Routine, ongoing technical programs for cross-border cooperation and sharing information are sensible and not captured by grandiloquent interpretations from the left and right. An example of such cooperation is a joint project between Natural Resources Canada's FleetSmart Program and the U.S. Environmental Protection Agency's SmartWay Transport Partnership to save fuel and reduce greenhouse gases from transport trucks. For those who worry that all of this is a slippery slope, this process is unlikely to give rise to new supranational government structures because the U.S. is inclined to a unilateralist approach to maintain and guard its prerogatives. We have seen this in 2006, when the U.S. only partially respected the decision of the dispute settlement mechanism on softwood lumber.

Was Free Trade Free?

In managing our relationship with the Americans, let's step back and ask, "Was free trade necessary? And what has its impact been?"

Too often we read unsupported statements like, "The Canadian economy was transformed by the Canada-U.S. Free Trade Agreement and later by the North American Free Trade Agreement."[4] In fact, it can be argued that the free trade agreements were not necessary as the rate of increase in trade between Canada and the U.S. before and after the agreements has been largely constant.[5]

The increase that came at the time of the first trade agreement was due to the low Canadian dollar. As one of the continentalists' leading advocates, economist Thomas Courchene writes, "The major undervaluation of the loonie with respect to the greenback prior to 2002 led to a three-fold increase in exports to the U.S."[6]

How necessary and significant were the FTAs? Consider this: before the first agreement in 1988, over 95 percent of trade moved tariff-free. The agreements affected the remaining 5 percent. As a point of information – the last of these tariffs ended without ceremony in January 2008.

And what about the argument that was used during the FTA debates – and again now, when a NAFTA-Plus is being advocated – that we need a strong regional trading bloc to compete in the world. It's an increasingly false premise – rhetoric from the continentalists. Does the world work on the basis of competing regional trading blocs? Increasingly, the world economy works on the basis of a global value-added production chain that can in part be regional but is also trans-regional, which is to say global.

I heard Tom d'Aquino, advancing the SPP as a NAFTA-Plus, say we must respond to the growing challenge from China and India by strengthening our ties with the U.S. Later the same day, Michael Ignatieff, running for the Liberal leadership, said

"China and India are getting so important we need to reduce our dependence on the U.S." The same facts can, and are, used to support opposite arguments and conclusions!

We didn't need free trade with Americans, and many of the arguments used to advance it and further integration with the U.S. are erroneous.

Trade with the Americans grew before and after the agreements. No matter the state of relations between the two countries, the value of our trade with each other tends to increase.

While we cannot forget that over 80 percent of our exports go to the U.S., 80 percent of our buying and selling of goods is within Canada. Our trade with the United States is one-sixth of combined internal and external Canadian trade. According to University of British Columbia economist emeritus, John F. Helliwell, trade among Canadians is still about ten times greater than trade between Canada and the U.S.[7]

Yet, as Mark Twain said, Canada and the U.S. are being drawn together by "invisible agencies." We are dealing with a force of nature; one that for the sake of Canada needs to be controlled and disciplined, not encouraged. Perhaps these agreements should be thought of as a shared recognition and psychological frame for what is happening.

Our relationship with the U.S. has a momentum of its own, based on massive and mutual self-interest. For Canada's part, we are largely focused upon and satisfied with selling to the American market. And why would we not be? The economy of just the U.S.'s Great Lakes states is 30 percent larger than China's.

The U.S. is contiguous with us — not thousands of miles and an ocean away with a different culture and a difficult foreign language. It has a GDP of almost $14 trillion, while China's economy, though much in the news, has a GDP of $2.6 trillion, or less than one-fifth that of the U.S. Its rate of growth is larger than the U.S., but the total increase per year is still much smaller than that of the U.S.

The Great Lakes states of New York, Pennsylvania, Illinois, Indiana, Michigan, Ohio, Wisconsin, and Minnesota have a regional GDP of almost $3.7 trillion U.S. That's over $1 trillion more than all of China.[8]

While it can be argued that the free trade agreements with U.S. were gilding the lily, it is hard to imagine that they would not have been signed. In the late 1980s and early 1990s, countries all over the world were entering into free trade agreements. Is it imaginable that with the U.S. signing an FTA with Mexico, that Canada would not have been at the table? In that context, is it plausible that two countries having a free trade agreement in the auto sector — the Auto Pact — would not have entered into a wider, free trade agreement?

Let's, for the sake of argument, agree that the FTAs didn't really have much impact on the growth of trade with the U.S. What impacts *did* they have? One is a partially functioning dispute resolution mechanism that gives us some, but not complete, satisfaction and the ability to say "You guys aren't living up to your agreement." I think that's worth something. The effect is on Canadian resolve more than anything. It also means that for those limited number of Americans who are listening, in their specialized niches, that they are put more on the defensive than they otherwise would be (even if this doesn't command instant results).

In the case of the softwood lumber dispute, while the ruling of the dispute settlement mechanism was not fully respected, the Harper government agreed to accept that $4 billion of the $5 billion unfairly extracted by U.S. tariffs be returned to Canadian producers. One could argue that the dispute settlement mechanism was 80 percent effective.

However, there is one sector where our free trade agreement with the Americans has significantly hurt us. As we will see in a future chapter on energy, Canada gave away its ability to shape policy in this critical sector. Instead, production and the evolving network of pipelines — while further developing the sector and making us rich — respond to American demand. This will mean that Canada will foolishly start to run out of gas and conventional oil, which has arguably already started to happen.

While I don't agree with what sometimes sounds like the fear mongering of the left-nationalists, on this big aspect of the Free Trade Agreement their worries are warranted. Part of the SPP concerns North American energy security. A leading opponent of current U.S. policy, retired U.S. Army Colonel Anne Wright, describes the Security and Prosperity Partnership as "Security and Prosperity Propaganda." In the energy sector, Colonel Wright is correct.

I find the disingenuousness of documents produced by the SPP concerning energy to be outrageous. They talk about supply to North American consumers and shortages faced by North American consumers, when what is really meant are shortages for Americans. Take this excerpt:

> The NAFTA has been instrumental in the emergence of an integrated North American market for energy goods. For trade between Canada and the United States, limits on the use of export restrictions and the narrowing in scope of the national security exception ensures that consumers have access to continental energy supplies.[9]

The words "ensures consumers access to continental energy supplies" means not "consumers" but U.S. consumers and not "access to continental energy supplies" but access to *Canadian* oil and gas. It does not refer, by the way, to Mexican oil and gas, as Mexico did not allow energy to be on the table when it negotiated NAFTA.

Moving beyond these serious concerns about oil and gas, the Free Trade Agreements have also created a new psychological reality. As the saying goes, "Perception is everything." As we perceive ourselves to have taken this big step, we now ask, "What is the next big step going to be, when are we going to take it, and how are we going to take it?" Do small steps now make taking a big step later easier and more likely? Perhaps we will take many small incremental steps that will eventually amount to a big step.

Perhaps the most significant of next big steps would be the free flow of citizens across the border as part of the logic of free trade, what's known as "labour mobility." With growing economic integration, companies increasingly have facilities in both countries, and to advance their operations they often need to move personnel. Which leads to statements like this: "I need Mary and Antonio in Cincinnati, they understand our systems in Toronto." There is a provision in the FTAs for intra-firm cross-border staff transfers, and it's logic could be expanded upon.

Once citizens are able to live and work freely in the two countries, the future will look very different. Countries are not just about the land, they're mostly about the people. If people mix and start to merge as one, then, in the fullness of time, Canada will much more quickly blend with the U.S.

Many of these big idea proposals come from economists who, from a narrow base of expertise, draw vast conclusions. A term like "labour mobility" left only in the hands of economists is a mistake. For them, labour mobility is within the logic of next steps like a customs union with common external tariffs. But as Michael Hart, one of the leading Canadian continentalist economists, perhaps uncharacteristically acknowledged at one conference, "You know I'm trying to learn more about political science and the other social sciences. My focus, my rationale for comment and certainty has been, and is, too narrow." I couldn't have put it better. The ramifications and significance of "labour mobility" is much larger than is its meaning for economists.

We must be wary of big solutions in our relations with the U.S.; free trade was not free, it has fuelled the forces of nature described by Mark Twain as "invisible agencies."

7
Rules for the Dance

Understanding the American way of politics and its impact on relations with Canada is so crucial that it is useful to review some of the highlights. Above all, one must never forget that the U.S. is a self-absorbed world unto itself at the centre of global issues. This means that what Canada does or does not do is of little significance to the American government. The U.S. makes decisions through a process more foreign to ours than we realize. In our system, the prime minister has only one constraint, the ability to get his decisions through Parliament. In a majority government, that is particularly easy.

In the U.S., its sheer size and scope combined with the division of powers among the president, the Congress, and the Judiciary mean building political capital in Washington is of limited value. Yet our pundits and politicians, including senior ministers, persist in misunderstanding this.

In the U.S., the issues that affect Canada are rarely linked. To paraphrase our former ambassador in Washington, Michael Kergin, "Think of at least three parts of the jungle — political, economic, and military. The three constituencies are different, be very skeptical of linkages between them."

We tend to forget that the U.S. needs Canada. Ours is not a relationship of one-way dependence. The Congress is full of all kinds of transborder, sectoral, and border state interests that want and need the continuation of good relations and the easy movement of goods and people across the border. Canada has lots of cards to play, so why underplay our hand? We are in a position to give ourselves much more freedom than we've allowed ourselves. As Eddie Goldenberg, a senior adviser to Prime Minister Chrétien, said to me, "Let's not negotiate against ourselves."

So the question is, "*Why* do we not manage our relations with the U.S. properly?" The answer is ideology, informed by a lingering colonial mentality. Part of our senseless left-right ideological polarization is a colonial habit of fighting for or against an imperial connection. Too much still passes through that lens. For example, we let the nationalist-left mindlessly shut down some political debates, such as those on health care, with the label "American-style." This anti-American, pro-American dichotomy is a disservice to ourselves.

Working on the coal face of this discussion, I have come to the conviction that we must take the best from the nationalist school — its counsel of caution — and the best from the continentalist school — its appreciation that our interests can be furthered through our relations with the U.S.

When a paradigm is about to shift, debate has a lack of reality to it, and advocates talk past each other. The realization that the U.S. did not care very much what Canada did and that our political leaders failed to understand this was initially what brought Janice Gross Stein and Eugene Lang together and led to their award-winning book, *The Unexpected War, Canada in Kandahar*. They write of Canada's decision not to participate in the American Ballistic Missile Defence Program:

> It was not terribly important to Washington, the
> Pentagon official said, whether Canada joined
> or not; Washington would not care much and
> Canada would pay no price for saying 'No.' The
> message was so counterintuitive, so different

from the heated rhetoric in Canada, so at odds with consensus within the federal government.[1]

We need a new paradigm, one perhaps recognized by Stein and Lang. Let us challenge the left and the right and their shared, old, post-colonial preoccupations.

The idea that Canada is a preternaturally vulnerable, timid mouse, and that congruent interests in the U.S. are not engaged, is not true. The U.S. is an elephant, but, when it comes to Canada, it is *not* in bed with a mouse.

All things considered, the elephant is in bed with a muskox that has some weight and heft of its own. We are a medium-sized country with the world's hegemonic power as our neighbour. It is not ideological to say that government is a crucial vehicle to articulate and advance our interests.

And consistent with all of this, let's not misunderstand the SPP. It is a post 9/11 attempt to put the problem of security into the context of prosperity and a continuation of the NAFTA process of moving toward closer economic relations. The SPP is an attempt to turn a problem into a partnership. Predictably, given the nature of our debate, it is both much less than what its right-continentalist boosters want and its left-nationalist detractors fear. It should rather be understood, and appreciated, as a neat piece of relationship management.

I accept the intention as described by the government:

> By appointing a Deputy Prime Minister with responsibilities over border management, Canada demonstrated its political commitment to ensuring a more secure but open border and underscored to American leaders and officials the importance Canada placed on the issue.[2]

The NAFTA and the SPP are not analogous to the European Union and its formation. There is almost no bureaucratic machinery in North American cooperation, unlike in the EU which is almost defined by it. What is happening in North America, despite boosters of the concept of a North American Community, is extremely far from a common market – the basic unit of the EU. The EU negotiates with the world as a bloc, the three NAFTA countries are never going to negotiate a NAFTA-China free trade agreement. For the NAFTA nations to do that they would first need a common external tariff and perhaps the internal free flow of people. Can anyone imagine the U.S. even contemplating the free flow of Mexicans into the U.S.? It's common especially for Europeans to mistake NAFTA for the EU; I did an interview with BBC World recently and despite my best efforts, was unable to convince them otherwise.

The EU has its basis in crisis and symmetries. The lack of both on this continent does not favour a North American Union. Europe suffered centuries of war and two devastating world wars within thirty years, from which a move towards union was a solution. In Europe, there have been symmetries such as France to balance Germany. In North America, the size, population, and power of the U.S. dwarfs that of Canada and Mexico. The EU has also never had to try and integrate such a populous country with such a disparity of wealth as Mexico. Finally, there is a community of relatively shared values in Europe that does not exist in North America. For the U.S., a social democratic philosophy, common in Europe and in Canada, is anathema.

In Canada, the nationalist left, for all its good intentions, and the continentalist right, for all its convictions, share what Lester Pearson has described in another context as a "psychological weakness." In accepting his Nobel Peace Prize, Pearson said, "The essential truth is that peace is merely the aggregate of feelings and emotions in the hearts and minds of individual people."[3]

I would argue that how we understand and engage the Americans is about the aggregate of feeling and emotions in the hearts and minds of Canadians.

Spokespeople for big business tell us we must do this and that in response to American threats. The admonishments are based, as we have seen, not so much on an understanding of how things work but on *fear*.

A leading left-nationalist, Michael Byers, in his *Intent for a Nation: What Is Canada For?*, describes how he left Canada for the U.S. disillusioned that we signed the free trade agreement, "Convinced that the country was finished."[4] In effect, he's saying "If you can't beat them, join them." But twelve years later, amazed Canada didn't join the war in Iraq or Ballistic Missile Defence, he returns. His basis for both leaving and returning involves a preoccupation with our vulnerability to the Americans.

Understanding how the U.S. works and how our relationship with them functions allows our actions to flow from old habits to a new paradigm.

Our exposure to the U.S. can leave us feeling small and insignificant. Too often we are shocked and hurt that Canada is at the margins of American consciousness. Why do we feel this way when the explanation is that the U.S. is absorbed by internal preoccupations and international hot spots?

Canada is a significant country in the world. We make an impact and contribute to the international community regardless of whether we are top of mind with the Americans, which we never are. When our reference is too exclusively American this can lead to a misunderstanding of how we fit most effectively in the clockwork of the international system, an important consideration to be explored in the chapter "Beyond Our Shared Continent, Canada in the World."

We need to define our interests and work with the U.S. to advance them, moving beyond "psychological weakness" based on fear. There is no solution other than sensible management and administration. If this relationship were a dance it would be called "Doing the Continental."

Part III
Dance Venues

8

What's Mexico Got to Do with It: Continental Counterweight or Deadweight?

"How best to engage the Americans?" is the central question of this book. One of the answers is to embrace Mexico as a continental counterweight.

This is consistent with the idea that if we deal with the Americans one-on-one — bilaterally — we are more vulnerable than if there are other parties at the table. And hence the Canadian belief, normally well founded, in what is called multilateralism. Yet, Mexico is, in reality, a deadweight.

The North American Free Trade Agreement of 1993 includes Mexico and was signed five years after the Canada-U.S. Free Trade Agreement. In fact, NAFTA is essentially two trade agreements — one between the United States and Canada, and one between the United States and Mexico — housed under one rubric.

Commerce between Canada and Mexico is a relatively insignificant 1.6 percent of total NAFTA trade, or $14 billion. In contrast, trade between Canada and the U.S. was $531 billion, while trade between Mexico and the U.S. was $330 billion. (All figures are in Canadian dollars.) Canada and Mexico each send much less than 5 percent of their exports to each other and more than 85 percent of their exports to the United States.[1]

While it is true that the small amount of Canada-Mexico trade has more than doubled since 1993, it is still relatively insignificant and should not lead to confusion about Mexico's importance to us.

It is perhaps a mistake, in the first instance, to understand Mexico as part of North America. To do so confuses analysis, gets us off track, and gives rise to thinking about Canada's future in North America rather than its future with the United States of America. Mexico's relevance to Canada is not direct, but secondary. Mexico's significance for Canada is only in the relevance Mexico has for the United States.

This is a critical point, an example of how our Canada-U.S. debate is framed incorrectly. Discussion of our future with the U.S. is usually characterized by unrealistic, extreme nationalist versus continentalist positions. It is also presented unhelpfully as involving Canada's future in North America, which is to say our future not just with the U.S. but also with Mexico.

As this book is about understanding Canada's relations with the Americans and about flagging what makes sense and what doesn't — placing too much emphasis on Mexico does not make sense

Two *New York Times* foreign correspondents, one posted to Canada and the other to Mexico, each wrote books in the same year about their postings that illustrate the chasm between the two countries. The reporter in Mexico wrote "Possibly nowhere in the world do two countries as different as Mexico and the U.S. live side by side." and the Canadian correspondent wrote "No two countries on the globe are as alike as Canada and the United States."[2]

Mexico is part of Latin America and more specifically part of Central America, with which it shares the Mayan and Aztec cultures. Arguably, Mexico has less in common with the neighbouring U.S. states of California and Texas than with Guatemala with which it was once part of colonial New Spain.

It is perhaps a misnomer to describe Mexico as part of North America — with all that implies — when Mexico is culturally more fully a part of Latin and Central America.

For some there has also been a sense that Canada and Mexico share more than they do. Author Anthony DePalma, in *Here: A Biography of the New American Continent*, argues the two countries are part of what he describes as a shared "here," when, in fact, they do not have a substantive complex relationship involving a rich weave of civil society interactions.[3]

The Canada-U.S. border is a demarcation of two industrial countries, while the U.S. border with Mexico is the longest land border between a Western and a developing country. And the problems one would expect along such a border are evident.

Profound differences distinguish Mexico from Canada and the United States. For example, 40 percent of the Mexican population of 100 million makes less than $3 a day CAD, and the vast majority of its farmers — normally described as peasants — could not rent or sell land until 1991.[4]

NAFTA was viewed as a way to further and deepen reforms begun by Mexico's leadership in the 1980s and 1990s. The U.S. has been supportive as it wants to draw Mexico into Western economic norms and practices. Democratization and a stable Mexico are in American economic interests for a number of reasons, including the importance of the country as its second largest supplier of oil.[5]

The growing Hispanic population in the U.S. is having an influence in turning attention in American politics to Latin America and more specifically to Mexico. This is reinforced by the movement of population generally to the southwest where the concentration of Mexican immigration is highest. Mexico and Canada are competitors for U.S. attention, and momentum is clearly not with Canada.

Canada and the U.S. and the U.S. and Mexico face different issues. There is little benefit in mixing these. Mexico is, for the most part, a complicating factor for Canada in its relations with the United States.

When significant elements of the Canadian business community advance expanding NAFTA they forget that many Americans and their leaders are not inclined to consider proposals without Mexican participation. Prospects for a Customs Union where the members have common external tariffs, often described as the next step for NAFTA, are greatly complicated by the fact that Mexico has free trade agreements with the European Union and with Japan.

In our relations with Washington, Mexico can be a source of confusion, a competing supplicant, a cautious ally, or an ally of the Americans.

A misplaced interest in trilateralism fuels the project of creating a North American Community. Many continentalists and nationalists would have us engage Mexico in a North American undertaking. Continentalists trying to advance closer relations with the U.S. argue that "we won't be alone with the Americans, it will be trilateral, you know, a kind of multilateralism, and I know you are not against multilateralism." Both camps in our polarized debate fall victim to similar notions; continentalists urge us to "lift NAFTA and put it on the road to a North American Community" and nationalists call on us to "work with our Mexican partner to build a North American community agenda."

Lloyd Axworthy, a leading left-Liberal and minister of foreign affairs from January 1996 to October 2000, has written that a "strong and inclusive partnership between Canada and Mexico is key" and that we should "work in concert and mesh our efforts in a potent combination to push for a North American community."[6] Axworthy helped to launch trilateral meetings of foreign ministers and establish a Canada-Mexico Commission, but both initiatives have been abandoned. Axworthy's vision, while attractive, is not realistic. Canada and Mexico assumed they were allies after the signing of the NAFTA in 1993 and there was a honeymoon. We have since learned that, more than anything, we compete for U.S. attention and that this rivalry mostly benefits the U.S.

Canada is concerned that its influence in Washington is declining while Mexico's is growing. During the 1990s, Mexico's trade with the U.S. doubled, and by the end of this decade may surpass Canada's trade with the U.S. We worry that the momentum of U.S. demographics with its burgeoning Hispanic population also favours Mexico and that these factors are leading to a shift in American priorities. This is reflected, for example, by President George W. Bush's decision to make his first foreign visit to Mexico rather than to Canada as had his three predecessors.

We share with Mexico an affinity, which is a wariness of the United States and can relate to the proverb: "Poor Mexico, so far from God, so close to the United States." We entertained the hope of tying down the hegemon together but sadly have discovered a common strategy is unrealistic and ineffective. As a Mexican foreign minister said: "Mexico and Canada cannot possibly make a sandwich; there is too much meat in between."[7]

Mexico has it's preoccupations with the U.S., and we have ours. There is little benefit in mixing these issues which moreover mislead us into imaging a tri-lateral community.

We should nurture our relationship with Mexico on the basis that we are advancing our links with Latin America through one of its leading members, rather than engaging Mexico to get the most out of our relations with the Americans.

Canada's belief in multilateralism would be justified only if NAFTA was to have many more members and morph into a Free Trade Area of the Americas (FTAA) — an initiative which is completely stalled. Yes, there is value in engaging the Americans in a community, but while it might start with Yukon it must extend beyond Yucatán.

9
An Energy Superpower Without an Energy Strategy

Energy, a driving force in our economy, forms a major part of our interaction with the United States. However, despite being both one of the world's largest energy producers and one of the world's largest energy exporters, Canada has no energy strategy in any meaningful, positive sense. Instead, Canada has an energy policy by default: we export as much oil and natural gas as we can to the U.S. We seek to maximize short-term export sales and help the U.S. meet its energy needs. Little, if any, attention is paid to Canada's future energy needs.

Meanwhile, the world is running out of oil and gas, largely because of increasing demand. The U.S. is running out of oil and gas even more quickly. It has turned to Canada to help make up the shortfall, and its needs are having a significant impact on our oil and gas industry. U.S. demand for Canadian oil and gas is spurring Canadian exploration and development, making Canadian energy company investors lots of money, creating lots of jobs, and increasing tax revenues. Sounds, as they say, like a "no brainer." A happy situation for all — or is it, in fact, a fool's paradise?

The first oil supply crisis came in the 1970s as Japan and Europe fully rejoined the international economy. The current one is happening as China, India, and a number of other developing countries are more fully entering the international economy.

In China alone, almost five million new vehicles are being added to the roads each year. Twenty-four of its thirty-one provinces are experiencing energy shortages. At the current rate of increasing demand, China will double its oil imports by 2012.[1]

The world currently consumes the equivalent of one Olympic size swimming pool filled with oil every fifteen seconds, or 86 million barrels a day. Demand rose by more than 1.8 million barrels a day in 2006. That increase represents about 70 percent of Canada's daily production of 2.6 million barrels per day. Even at today's level of demand, every drop of the world's known conventional reserves will be extracted in about thirty-seven years.[2]

For the first hundred years of oil production, until the mid-1950s, the U.S. produced twice as much oil as any other country. Still the world's third largest oil producer, the U.S. now *imports* two-thirds of its oil, with demand expected to double by 2020.[3] It currently uses more than 20 million barrels a day, or one-quarter of the worlds daily production.[4]

Canada is now the Americans' largest source of imported oil, more than 1.6 million barrels a day.[5] In other words, almost one in ten cars on U.S. highways has its tank full of Canadian gas.

While the U.S. is dependent on imported oil, it is more self-sufficient when it comes to other sources of energy. It is the world's largest producer of coal and natural gas. Yet even for natural gas, it imports about 15 percent of its needs, almost all of which comes from Canada. Half of the natural gas produced in Canada goes across the border.[6]

Importing oil and gas in 2004 cost the Americans more than U.S. $660 million a day — one third of the daily U.S. trade deficit of $2 billion. The cost to the U.S. of Canadian oil and gas exports in 2004 was well over $100 million a day, which is more than $36 billion annually.[7]

To evaluate if our U.S. energy exports make economic and political sense, we need to first understand Canadian energy production and supply. As both the world's fifth largest producer and exporter of energy from all sources,[8] Canada is an energy superpower. We are the world's ninth largest oil producer. We are the world's third largest producer of natural gas and the second largest exporter of natural gas after Russia.[9]

Our oil and natural gas exports have gone up 450 percent since the early 1980s.[10] From many perspectives, this increase is a positive development. There are, however, some concerns. Our production of conventional oil is dropping, and almost half of the oil we now produce comes from Alberta's tar sands. But to extract a barrel of oil from the sands requires an immense amount of hot water, currently heated by natural gas. In fact, it takes the equivalent in natural gas of one-third of a barrel of oil to produce a barrel of tar sands oil. And the three barrels of water which are heated to produce that barrel of tar sands oil become polluted.

At current projected rates of production and export, Canada has only ten years of proven natural gas reserves remaining. Natural gas is an efficient, clean-burning fuel. Does it make sense to use it to produce the world's dirtiest oil? By 2020, industry experts estimate that Canadian production of tar sands oil will triple to more than three million barrels per day. This will require huge amounts of increasingly scarce natural gas. In fact, it is widely understood that all of the natural gas flowing through a new pipeline from the Mackenzie River Delta would be required. Imagine, the gas from a huge $10 billion pipeline, one of the world's largest construction projects, moving natural gas from one of the world's last and largest reserves used for tar sands oil production — and not to heat millions of homes in Canada and, indeed, the U.S.

You know energy is running short when it is extracted increasingly from remote locations and non-conventional sources. Moving natural gas from the Arctic to produce oil from tar sands is a signal example of dwindling reserves of accessible conventional energy.

Converting natural gas, so versatile and clean, into heavy oil is reverse alchemy. Is this the best way to use our limited reserves of natural gas? Is this in Canada's interest?

The increase in our natural gas and oil exports has been very lucrative for Canada, but the time has arrived to re-assess the situation. Are we, in this dimension of our relationship with the United States, making realistic decisions based on a rational understanding of our strengths and challenges? Are our objectives realistic? Should we have other priorities than making as much money as possible in the short term? We are certainly not spurning the Americans — are we unnecessarily and foolishly embracing them?

In short, is our behaviour in our national interest?

Most countries feel it is important and legitimate to have an energy policy. In this country, one could argue that we have not articulated such a strategy. Rather, we have a de facto policy of supplying the Americans with as much oil and natural gas as we can produce.

In response to the high energy prices of the late 1970s and 1980s, the federal government adopted the National Energy Program (NEP) of price controls and export taxes. The goal was to protect Canadian consumers from rapid price increases. But the NEP was so reviled in oil-producing Alberta that a role for government today in the oil and gas sector has been rejected.

As a result, our oil and gas industry has become an extension of the American market. This is an example of the trap this country falls into when debate is influenced by two extremes: reject the Americans or embrace them. The NEP, in part, is a manifestation of the former and the current situation reflects the other pole. This extremism is foolish. In this domain of our relations with the Americans we are succumbing to a weakness in our collective psychology.

Virtually all of our energy exports go to the U.S. and account for 27 percent of total U.S. energy imports. Our U.S. exports of oil and natural gas began to increase rapidly in 1980, but have recently levelled off. Exports of oil over the past twenty-five years increased by 455 percent.[11] Exports of natural gas increased by 444 percent.[12] All were distributed through a huge new transborder pipeline infrastructure. Pipelines "hard-wire" relationships like nothing else, and this dramatic expansion happened without our collective awareness — without discussion, let alone debate.

Today, our production of conventional crude is declining, though exports of oil will likely continue to grow due to increased production from the tar sands. For natural gas, our exports to the U.S. have declined 13 percent since 2000 due to our limited supply of less than ten years of proven reserves at current rates of production. And yet we remain the second largest exporter of natural gas in the world. North America, until recently self-sufficient in natural gas, is increasingly importing liquid natural gas from such places as Trinidad and Russia.[13]

Natural gas economically and cleanly heats millions of homes during our long, cold winters. Does it make sense to export half of our production, and then use new supplies from the Canadian Arctic to produce oil for export from the tar sands?

We clearly need a debate about the management of our energy reserves. It must be a rational debate. One that considers the pan-Canadian national interest. One that does not rely on and succumb to foolish and unhelpful ideologies where pundits employ rhetoric and name calling. One that goes beyond the shibboleths of neo-conservatism versus socialism. And, most importantly, a debate which is not framed as either embracing or rejecting the Americans.

Let's remember as we engage this discussion that the value of Canadian natural gas exports to the U.S. in 2004 was about $25 billion and oil was about $9 billion[14]; a significant part of our $77 billion trade surplus with the U.S.[15] The value to the Canadian economy of current levels of exploration and production for use domestically and for export to the U.S. is $75 billion per year.[16] Great for the oil patch, but not so great for Canadian manufacturers. As a result of these lucrative exports on a massive scale the value of the Canadian dollar has gone up. But this is hard on our manufacturing sector — making what it produces more expensive to foreign buyers. To what extent is our trade surplus with the U.S. enhanced by an increase in energy exports, and to what extent is it diminished by a decline in manufacturing exports?

In Ottawa, the U.S. Embassy website points out that our energy exports contribute to our trade surplus with the Americans. It seems very unlikely that we will ever find data from the American government indicating how much our trade surplus with them is reduced by a decline in our manufacturing exports. The Americans have an American national interest, and they are certainly not afraid to articulate and advance it.[17]

Why should we not sensibly assess *our* national interest? We don't say the U.S. is being anti-Canadian when it marshals data to advance its interests. Why should we feel we are being anti-American in determining *our* interest? Determining and advancing our national interests can and must be separate from being anti-American. Sometimes our national interests are in sync with American national interests, and at other times they may diverge.

The time has come to consider an energy strategy for Canada, one allowed to diverge from the American national interest. At the moment, our energy resources are subsumed within the framework of North American energy security. For example, we have declared ourselves partners with the U.S. in realizing the self-sufficiency objectives of its National Energy Policy.

The U.S. National Energy Policy of 2001 was articulated by the White House and lead by Vice President Dick Cheney. Canada formally works to achieve security of supply through the

North American Energy Working Group of the Security and Prosperity Partnership of North America.

Since Canada does not currently have an energy supply problem, there is insufficient pressure for us to define our interests. That makes it easier to respond positively to American imperatives. However, what will happen when we run out of conventional oil and use the last of our natural gas reserves to produce oil from the tar sands?

We are encouraged by the U.S. to work together for North American energy security when what we are really responding to is U.S. energy insecurity — to the U.S. national interest. But is this in our own national interest? Is it anti-American? Is it disloyal to articulate our own interests, accepting that they might not be in harmony with U.S. interests?

However, in answering these questions we must be mindful that the world's economies, and especially the Canadian and U.S. economies, are so interconnected that if the American economy is threatened by energy insecurity so is our economy and so is global prosperity. Nevertheless, Canada clearly has a strong energy hand to play and should not be afraid to pursue its interests.

There is also the issue and challenge in Canadian domestic politics of natural resources being a provincial jurisdiction, and that Alberta's short-term interests are well served by the current arrangement. Western Canada in Canadian history, and with reason, has developed a sense of alienation and subjugation to the populous provinces of Ontario and Quebec. After Ottawa's NEP of the 1980s, when Alberta felt it was diminished,[18] it has become a third rail of Canadian politics to challenge the current status quo on energy policy. We need to be able to have a rational debate about energy policy that allows us to manage our resources in a sensible way without holding Alberta back.

The Alberta government is satisfied with the current situation. The American government, for reasons we've examined, is also content with the current arrangements. So while Canadian and American interests in this domain of their relationship may not be coterminous, Alberta's perception of its interests — nurtured in Canadian history and within the relatively short time frames of business and politics — are largely congruent with the needs of the United States.

This is the challenge for Canada in arriving at a sensible understanding of our energy production, exports and reserves. Our desire to work with and accommodate the needs of our North American partner and our made-in-Canada domestic political considerations combine to constrain us in articulating and advancing our true interests.

A massive north-to-south pipeline distribution system has been built in the last decade to carry the almost five-fold increase in exports of oil and natural gas. This increase is due to the North American Free Trade Agreement. Under NAFTA, Canadian suppliers must charge U.S. customers the same prices as Canadian buyers, and exports are not restricted. We now send two thirds of the oil and half of the natural gas we produce to the U.S.

Under the proportionality clause of NAFTA, those percentages are locked in.[19] In other words, if we are faced with a domestic shortage, we cannot divert U.S. exports to Canada. This was the crunch clause we traded for the Americans agreeing to respect their own trade laws. This commitment to be enforced by the rulings of a dispute settlement process has not been respected by the Americans in the softwood lumber dispute; a cause for much outrage and discussion in Canada. Yet, in a time of severely declining global, North American, and national energy reserves, our huge increase in exports has happened with little collective awareness and without a trace of debate.

For oil and gas, the elephant in the room is NAFTA. It is due to NAFTA that exports have grown so dramatically. If there is nothing we could have done to slow the growth of these exports, perhaps it is understandable that there has been little discussion. We had the debate — it happened during the Free Trade Election of 1988 when the Brian Mulroney Conservatives won with 42 percent of the vote, and we are living with the aftermath of that decision.

But energy exports need to be considered in light of the reserves necessary for Canada's future needs.[20] The legacy of the NEP — "Let the eastern bastards freeze in the dark" — and increasing percentages of our production exported to the U.S. under NAFTA will mean that all Canadians may one day freeze in the dark.

There is also a lack of awareness and debate about electricity exports. Though this was for a time, of course, not the case after August 14, 2003, when a tree branch fell on a transmission line in Ohio. Within six minutes, sixty-two thousand megawatts went offline in eight U.S. states, including the twenty-one thousand megawatts that Ontario normally uses each day.

In Canada electricity is largely generated by the provinces. There is some connection between provincial electricity grids, but the trend is toward three north-south North American regional grids that are coming to operate under U.S. federal government regulation. The U.S. Administration's National Energy Policy includes electricity in its goal of a seamless North American energy market. However, electricity is an element of our energy trade which is not subject to the NAFTA proportionality clause. As a result, we have an opportunity in our electricity trade to find the right balance between embracing or rejecting the Americans.

The NEP, the ideological climate in Alberta, and NAFTA have moved us away from public intervention, but there is now an expanding debate about sustainable and managed growth that puts the government back into play. A Conservative prime minister from Alberta would be in a position to lead such a debate — which would be much more difficult for a Liberal or NDP prime minister, or for a Conservative prime minister not from western Canada.

To realize our energy potential, we need to develop a framework embracing all the different elements of the energy sector — oil, gas, nuclear, hydro. Such an energy strategy would encourage the upgrading of bitumen from the oil sands in Canada rather than exporting it to the U.S. to be upgraded there. Nuclear energy could be used to produce the steam to remove the sand from the tar rather than natural gas, and it would reduce carbon emissions.

Energy policy may now be emerging as part of concern about the environmental impact of expanding tar sands oil production. There is clearly a tension between U.S. security of oil supply and President Obama's commitment to reduce the impact of dirty sources of energy in the fight against global warming.

The economic downturn of late 2008 and 2009 gives us a good opportunity to pause and consider sustainable managed growth in the interest of the environment, the economy, and society. This, however, needs some direction. Market mechanisms are not sorting this out, nor is it likely that they can. These issues go beyond the market and decisions of business people. Through discussion, society has to articulate goals and governments will have to show some leadership to meet the challenges, enabling us to realize the full potential of our energy sector.

The idea that we are dependent on the U.S., and at the right moment must be supplicants for a new grand bargain, is foolish and misguided. It is based on a misunderstanding, by influential elements of our society, that we have a one-way dependency upon and vulnerability to the U.S. In fact, the two countries need each other. It is not just Canada that is dependent on this relationship. We need to make rational decisions based on the reality of our relations. The world's most voracious energy consumer needs us.

China, with its 1.3 billion inhabitants and almost 10 percent per year economic growth, is also looking to Canada for energy. The Chinese government oil company PetroChina and Canada's Enbridge have agreed to build a $2.5 billion, 1,200-kilometre pipeline to carry oil from the tar sands to the B.C. coast for export. As such, China should be a negotiating point with the Americans; it represents, for the first time, the possibility of diversifying our trade in at least the resource sector.

One of the central arguments of this book is that we tend to either mindlessly embrace or reject the United States. If in the case of the Avro Arrow we mindlessly rejected its offer to pay for the planes, in the case of our energy relations we are mindlessly embracing the U.S. In both cases our interests have not been furthered to the extent possible.

For oil and gas exports we have become part of the American oil and gas market. We are thus subject to the logic of that market, which is to address U.S. supply shortage. Imagine a Canada short of natural gas and obliged under the proportionality clause of the NAFTA to send 80 percent of our production to the U.S. We may have to reopen the NAFTA or abrogate it, which we can do with six months notice. Our trade in electricity and how we develop the tar sands is less constrained and more readily amenable to the innovation which must come from renewed discussion and debate.

We do not need to tempestuously reject or, like a vassal state, subordinate our needs to the United States. Let us articulate the national interest and advance it. We expect no more or less from our American partners. We need action now to launch a new debate — balanced and sensible — about the development and export of our dwindling energy reserves.

10
Not Watertight

Everybody I spoke to about this book told me, "Yes, water! You have to talk about water!" Yet my feeling was that while perhaps looming as a transcendent issue in binational relations, water is largely a regional and local concern.

Water is a fine example of effective management in Canadian-American relations, and current fears of sharing it with the U.S. are somewhat irrational.

How is it that we export without restriction as much oil and gas to the U.S. as we possibly can, and at the same time have a huge fear of selling a drop of water?

Water's place in our relationship with the U.S. is informed by a number of factors: the global water context, water use in the U.S., how much water there actually is in Canada, cross-border water management, and NAFTA. In the end, are water and energy really so different?

As in the chapter on energy, let's look first at the global context. The United Nations says more than 450 million people, in over thirty countries, face shortages of fresh water. This number will increase to over 2.8 billion people by 2025. For the moment, worldwide bulk export of water by tanker is limited to sales from Turkey to Cyprus and Israel.[1]

To mark the urgency of these issues, a World Water Day is observed each year; associated concerns about global warming preoccupy us. Polar ice is melting, and there is speculation that one result will be a weakening of the Gulf Stream that warms and waters Western Europe.

Within this context of gathering crisis is a sense that the U.S. is running out of water and is looking to Canada to quench its thirst. What is the situation with water in the U.S.? Until the 1970s, the rate of U.S. GDP growth and water consumption tracked each other closely, giving the impression our neighbour was heading for massive water shortages.

However, since the 1980s water use has stabilized and even declined. Two things happened — conservation and desalination. Leading observers now write, "A very strong technical argument can be made that for the foreseeable future, U.S. water needs can be met domestically, and that the situation should not be considered desperate anytime soon."[2]

There are over twenty desalination plants in the U.S., mostly in California but also in Florida and Texas. They produce water for urban use at only twice the cost of conventional sources.

However, dry farming regions require too much water and are too distant from such plants to make desalination a feasible solution. The most dramatic example of the demands of irrigation is on the Colorado River, which flows from the western mountains and is drained so completely for farming as it runs through seven southwestern states that it no longer reaches the sea.

Another concern is groundwater. There may be more water underground than on the surface and together these sources form a hydrological system. Almost half of Americans, 140 million, depend on ground water. Demand has lead to over pumping. The continent's largest aquifer, High Plains or Ogallala, sits under eight Great Plains states and is the leading source of water to irrigate about one-quarter of all U.S. farmland. Most authorities feel this aquifer is being drained beyond the level of natural replenishment. Clearly, this has implications for Canada.

Aquifers are not well understood. We don't know how much water they contain: in fact, the largest may also extend under

Saskatchewan. Part of the North American hydrological system, aquifers are an element of the movement and management of transborder water.

How much water does each country have? The short answer is they have about the same amount of water available to them. The forty-eight continental states and the watersheds in Canada that do not flow to the Arctic each receive about 2.6 percent of the world's precipitation: what is often described as renewable water.[3]

This is a far cry from having 25 percent of the world's water at our disposal, a share that Canada is often erroneously thought to have. How can popular perception be so wrong?

Much of Canada was covered by two kilometres of glacial ice until about ten thousand years ago. The legacy of the last ice age is not only scoured rock, but the water from the ice that once abraded the rock.

We have lots of lakes in Canada because the glaciers melted and water filled many depressions, and we have relatively low evaporation rates. While the largest repository, the Great Lakes contain 18 percent of the world's fresh water, and only 1 percent of that falls each year as precipitation. To take more than 1 percent from the Great Lakes is to drain them of their water capital from the last Ice Age. The water in the Great Lakes is largely a non-renewable inheritance from that time.

While we have less renewable water available to us than we normally realize, this does not mean we should not consider sharing or selling any of it.

Why not move more water within and between watersheds? In fact, we do both already. It is certainly less momentous than some of the things we have done and are doing to the environment. For example: over the last two centuries we have cut down inconceivably large forested areas and drained more than half of the Prairie wetlands. Virtually no water now leaves the Colorado River and the Rio Grande, which clearly must have a huge impact on the Pacific Ocean. Currently, we bring in fresh water from every corner of the world in the holds of ships as ballast and dump it directly unfiltered into the Great Lakes from which zebra mussels and other invasive species move through rivers and canals and into other lakes.

It is also not widely appreciated that we already move water between watersheds in North America. There is more water going into than out of the Great Lakes because of two dams in Ontario, north of Lake Superior. These dams divert water, formerly heading to Hudson Bay, south to the Great Lakes. This is to compensate in part for water sent south from Lake Michigan at Chicago and ultimately to the Mississippi River. The two Canadian dams (built in the early 1940s) divert about 160 cubic metres per second into the Great Lakes; the diversion from Lake Michigan is about 90 cubic meters per second.[4] We also redirect huge amounts of water within Canada for hydroelectricity.

The argument that water should not move between watersheds due to concerns about "ecological integrity" sounds "scientific" and is used to try and close off debate. Surely, with millions of dollars of filters, including micro screening, we might consider moving more water between rivers and watersheds. The logic against doing so is perhaps not water tight.

The first example of effective water management and cooperation between the two countries emerged in response to a water dispute between Alberta and Montana. In 1901, Montana farmers planned to divert water between two rivers that crossed the border. Two years later, Alberta farmers starting digging a canal to recapture the water. In 1909, the International Joint Commission (IJC) was created to settle such disputes.

The IJC is an offshoot of the Canada-U.S. Boundary Waters Treaty that sets out procedures that are in part based on the principle that no waters flowing across the border shall be polluted on either side to the detriment or injury of the other party.

Our joint good-neighbour policy has so far dealt with over one hundred cases along the almost nine thousand kilometre Canada-U.S. border, of which nearly four thousand kilometres contain about four hundred rivers, streams, and lakes.

As in so many things, Canada and the U.S. inescapably cooperate. On a small scale, five neighbouring border communities share water: Vancouver and Point Roberts, Washington; Coutts, Alberta, and Sweetgrass, Montana; Gretna, Manitoba, and Neche, North Dakota; and St. Stephen, New Brunswick, and Calais, Maine.

Sometimes disputes are resolved in what might seem to be Canada's favour. On the Alberta-Montana border, the site of the first IJC-resolved dispute, the two rivers concerned, the Milk and the St. Mary, currently provide irrigation to 190,000 hectares of Alberta farmland and to 49,000 hectares in Montana.[5]

There are, of course, current water issues in the U.S. that concern us, such as safely diverting water from Devils Lake in North Dakota, which has no natural drainage, into Manitoba and then on to Hudson Bay. Another is the Garrison Dam, responsibly moving water from the Missouri River (part of the Mississippi River system) north to irrigate semi-arid regions in North Dakota.

In the Devils Lake case we agreed to the diversion. The agreement of 2005 provides flood relief in North Dakota while protecting Manitoba's waterways through testing and other precautions — particularly a system of filters.

The U.S. also has water issues with *us* that are managed through the IJC and of which Canadians are less aware than of the "outrages against us." There is concern that pollution will flow into Washington State from a Teck Cominco Limited smelter in British Columbia and fear of downstream pollution in Montana's famous Glacier National Park from possible drilling in British Columbia for coal bed methane.

Climate change is a shared concern in the North American west where many rivers (such as the St. Mary and the Colorado) have their source in mountain snow fields. These glaciers hold precipitation that is released into rivers during the summer, making their flow more even and useful.

With global warming, more rain is falling in winter, leaving less water to flow in summer. Dams may have to be built to hold the water for summer use. To give a sense of the scope of the potential problem, half of California's needs are met by water currently held in snow and ice fields during winter.

Another area of joint water management is the Columbia River. It, too, illustrates the interrelated realities of the two countries. In 1963, the U.S. Supreme Court put restrictions on how much water could be taken from the Colorado River, which is completely in the U.S. and is the next major river system south of the Columbia River. This decision meant there was increased demand for water from the Columbia River, which has its origins in Canada and its outlet to the Pacific in the U.S. Six years after the U.S. judicial decision concerning the Colorado River, the two governments signed the Columbia River Treaty, which, in part, transfers water from the Columbia River to the Colorado River basin.

The biggest example of continental water management in the world is the Great Lakes. Containing the largest bodies of fresh water on earth, the basin is also home to 43 million people. Stewardship of this shared resource falls under the IJC and other structures such as the Great Lakes Commission whose members are the eight Great Lakes states along with Ontario and Quebec. Other vehicles of shared management include the Great Lakes Water Quality Agreement and the Great Lakes Binational Toxics Strategy.

Some of the anxiety over exports of water to the U.S. has its basis in a 1998 application by a Canadian company, which was initially approved to export water by tanker from Lake Superior. Also in the same year there was a proposal to export even more water by tanker from a lake in Newfoundland.

The Lake Superior application caused a sensation in both Canada and the U.S. One result is the 2008 binational Great Lakes–St. Lawrence River Basin Water Resource Compact, which largely prohibits new water diversions. Another response was to amend the Boundary Waters Treaty to give the minister of foreign affairs authority to prohibit bulk water removals from boundary waters within Canadian jurisdiction.

The concept of selling water in bulk is now with us. It is happening in the Mediterranean and was proposed in Canada. This has rightfully led people to see the sale of water within the context of NAFTA. In the final agreement, water is not explicitly excluded as a tradable good, as it had been in earlier drafts.

The danger is that if we do sell water, it then becomes a commodity under NAFTA rules, and we know what that means for energy. Canadian oil and gas are now understood as part of "continental energy security" in which they are used for "optimum continental utilization." Let's be clear that the use of the word "continental" has nothing to do with Mexico. It has only and everything to do with the United States. Do we want water to fall into this same conceptualization and language of continentalization?

I think the answer is no. But by the same token, is it not possible to find a happy medium. We need something a little more rational, rather than exporting all the oil and gas we can but not a drop of water. An additional problem with such a stance on water is that we already manage water in ways that have significant continental dimensions.

The global and North American water context has led to a call for a national water strategy. Something, ironically, we have so far been unable to contemplate for energy.

Given the impetus of growing integration with the U.S., there is likely some momentum to include water in the framework of a continental conceptualization and for its commoditization. A chief "push-back" is to advance water as a fundamental human right, and it is urged that a national water strategy "would declare water a human right and protect rivers, lakes and groundwater from privatization, bulk exports and trade agreements."[6]

There is a sense that energy and water are dramatically different. That oil and gas are, absolutely, commodities and that water is absolutely not. In fact, they have similarities and differences.

Especially in colder climates like Canada's, energy and water are essential to human survival. Water and energy are used in countless industrial processes and in the generation of electricity. Water, oil, and natural gas under pressure are liquids. When an aquifer is exhausted by over pumping, how different is that from emptying an oil or gas well? So to the extent that water is not renewable, why not treat it like oil and gas? There is a growing shortage of both water and energy. Existentially, and in a more practical definition, life is energy.

Yet we are chemically 98 percent water, but (hopefully) zero percent petrochemicals. Water is the basis of all life, not just human life. Human survival depends on water while we only *need* energy. There are lots of different kinds of energy that can be substituted for each other. In most cases, there is no substitute for water.

Our rivers are key to understanding our history. And, water is not just in our lakes and rivers — it is in the land and part of the air, so much a component of the environment that it is not seen, as oil and gas, as a commodity.

Canadians are wary of, and emotional about, selling water as it is part of our national identity and the stuff of life. But we are already managing water on a continental basis. To actually sell a small fraction of some of the 60 percent of Canadian water that flows unheralded into James and Hudson Bays and elsewhere into the Arctic is not committing national hari-kari. Freezing in the dark because we've foolishly sold all of our oil and gas to the Americans is a more immediate and real threat.

The former esteemed and long-time premier of Alberta, Peter Lougheed, recently made a large and surprising splash with an opinion piece in the *Globe and Mail*.[7] No other figure so fully supports the transfer of our energy to the U.S., so it was a surprise when he wrote that under no circumstances should we sell the Americans water. "It would be a major mistake for Canada to handle this badly." Lougheed wrote. Such sweet, dripping irony — to never sell water while locked into exporting ever-increasing amounts of oil and gas to the U.S., currently more than 50 percent of our production.

We are blocked by the legacy of our National Energy Policy of the 1980s and the resulting impasse in domestic politics that benefits the U.S., as some canny American observers must surely appreciate.

Yet, if part of our reason for selling so much energy to the U.S. is to support the U.S. economy, which in turn supports the Canadian economy, to dramatically reduce exports would be to "cut off our nose to spite our face." If this argument holds for energy, surely it applies as well for water. To send water to the U.S. would also support the American economy and in turn support ours.

It makes no sense to avoid a national energy strategy to ensure we *sell* as much oil and gas to the U.S. as possible while embracing a national water strategy to ensure we *do not sell* any water to the U.S. What does make sense are national energy and water strategies based on our national interest; not upon our emotions and ideologies.

Opinion and government policy are quite nationalistic concerning water, yet are not so for oil and gas.

As suggested at the outset of this chapter, our relations with the U.S. concerning water are characterized by a long and solid history of cooperation and continuity rather than by instability and change.

There have been huge schemes for massive transfers of water to the U.S. These were imagined in response to rapid increases in U.S. water consumption that have since stabilized.

These schemes, from the 1960s and 1970s, involve damning the mouth of James Bay to create a freshwater reservoir, redirecting Arctic rivers and pumping water from Great Bear and Great Slave Lakes — projects along eastern, central, and western corridors that would cost more than $500 billion each. Put in perspective, they are massively bigger than the largest capital project under serious consideration in North America: the $10 billion Alaska oil pipeline. Suggesting that such water schemes are at all likely has the alarmist ring of an eight-lane NAFTA superhighway through Mexico, the United States, and Canada.

There are shortages of water for irrigation in dry U.S. agricultural regions, but the cost of transporting water to them from Canada is prohibitive. Currently, water supplied to the U.S. southwest costs less than $100 per acre-foot (the amount to cover one acre with one foot of water). Water delivered from Canada could not be done for less than $1,000 per acre-foot.[8] This is a statistic never mentioned by left-nationalists when they sometimes foster fear and anxiety in our relations with the U.S. and when, in fact, we are a long way from such grandiose schemes. The ideological polarization observed and discussed elsewhere in this book is also alive and well in our perception of water in our relationship with the Americans.

Yet when it comes to water, even with grand projects aside, Canada and the U.S. are more than in any other dimension of their relationship part of the "same piece of real estate."

11
Defrosting Arctic Sovereignty

Canada is not usually thought to be very nationalistic. When it comes to the Arctic, as "true north strong and free" in our anthem suggests, our patriotism is accentuated. Canadian leaders have launched elections with plans to develop the Arctic, and others win votes saying they will defend it.

We work with the U.S. in so many areas, but when it comes to the Arctic there is a sense that "This is about sovereignty. We are not going to be pushed around," and our starting point and collective reflex is distrust.

There is an understanding that our sovereignty is also challenged by our other Arctic neighbours, Russia and Denmark, through its possession of Greenland. The extent of a challenge from Russia concerns the scientific delimitation of continental shelves. With Denmark, the dispute is over Hans Island – a few acres of rock in the High Arctic between Baffin Island and Greenland.

To put our "sovereignty reflex" in context we need to appreciate that beyond miniscule Hans Island there is *no* challenge to Canada's sovereignty over the Arctic Islands.

Almost all the water and ice between the islands are accepted as internal Canadian waters and as completely within our jurisdiction. Disagreement is most pointedly with the U.S. over whether the Northwest Passage is Canadian internal waters. Besides this dispute, the only other Arctic sovereignty issue with the U.S. involves our shared boundary in the Beaufort Sea north of Yukon and Alaska.

This unsettled claim is over a wedge-shaped part of the Beaufort Sea and the seabed beneath it that likely holds oil and natural gas. The basis for our different assertions are quite technical and common with neighbouring countries.

The Northwest Passage is the dramatic, central issue in our Arctic relations with the U.S. The U.S. holds that the Passage is an international straight through which the ships of any nation may pass, while we say the Passage is part of our internal waters and that ships from other countries must have our permission to transit.

Part of the reason I'm writing this book stems from the first modern transit through the passage by the American oil super tanker, the *Manhattan*, in 1969.[1] It did so initially without Canada's permission, yet was assisted by the Canadian Coast Guard Ice Breaker *Sir John A. Macdonald*.

The transit of the *Manhattan* was at the heart of an innovative teaching model in my grade six class. Using daily newspapers as the starting point, we pursued learning about many topics from the Arctic to pollution, the sea to ships, and international relations and beyond. It was a fascinating way to be introduced to a wide range of subjects. As for many Canadians, the *Manhattan* helped to shape my initial impression of our relations with the U.S. and of the challenges they posed in the Arctic.[2]

Canada's response to the *Manhattan* was the Arctic Waters Pollution Prevention Act (AWPPA) of 1970, imposing safety and environmental requirements on all shipping within one hundred nautical miles of our Arctic coast. This is a little like a "we have a speed limit, but please let us know if you're speeding" regulatory regime through which we welcome responsible passage.[3]

The next challenge to our interpretation of the Northwest Passage as our internal waters came in 1985 with the transit of the U.S. Coast Guard Ship *Polar Sea*.

While these two voyages are often viewed as deliberate provocations, it is a mistake to see them in such certain terms.

As we saw previously, the U.S. rarely acts as a single coordinated unit. The passage of the *Polar Sea* is a perfect example. As a former American ambassador to Canada put it, "The *Polar Sea* went through as a Coast Guard initiative without consulting the U.S. government; it's a good example of how the U.S. government works. And there are other examples of a massive lack of coordination in the U.S. system."[4]

The U.S. has the only blue water navy in all of the world's oceans and is concerned that narrow passages through which it's navy and global shipping move be considered international and not internal waters. The U.S. is involved in a much bigger undertaking than setting out to specifically challenge Canada in the Northwest Passage.

Such passages are of strategic importance. The Strait of Malacca between Malaysia and Indonesia is perhaps the most notable, due, in part, to the oil tankers which pass from the Middle East on their way to Japan.

To assert its position on international passages, the U.S. in the 1980s sent warships into the Gulf of Sidra off the coast of Libya to contest an internal waters claim by that country. And, in 1986 the U.S. sent two warships into the Black Sea inside the twelve mile limit that the Soviet Union claimed as internal waters.

In response to the *Polar Sea* transit, Canada and the U.S. signed the 1988 Arctic Cooperation Agreement that "without prejudice to either sides legal position," the U.S. would seek Canadian permission to go through the Northwest Passage and that Canada would always answer in the affirmative — a joint don't agree, don't challenge policy.

We worked together to save face and achieve separate objectives through legal ambiguity that servers both countries. Climate change and melting ice are taking the Agreement out of its bilateral context, making transit by vessels from other countries more likely. Before global warming and melting polar ice, there was little interest from other countries in using the Passage – a time when ice can be seen to have been our ally.[5]

This new "climate" is a concern not only for Canada but also for the U.S. – and our informal agreement is unlikely to be enough for much longer. The U.S. is preoccupied with North American security and it is now in the U.S. interest for there to be a regulatory regime above the continent and throughout all of the Arctic waters. As the great bulk of these, including the Northwest Passage, are within Canada, who better, many in Washington ask, to provide and enforce such a regime than their continental ally.[6] That aircraft from any nation can fly above an international strait fuels support in the Pentagon for Canadian leadership.

Remember, the decision-making process in the U.S. involves a series of tribes and sub-tribes. And within that context some of Washington's tribes have a lot of sympathy for Canada to lead a Northwest Passage regulatory regime. This is an opportune juncture for Canada to achieve a jurisdictional role over the Passage not previously thought to be in the U.S. global interest.[7]

While the Passage has been a problem in our relations with the U.S., the current juncture indicates we may be on the cusp of a solution!

Somewhere between an international strait and internal waters we have to find the best possible regulatory regime for us to administer. If we insist on the internal waters concept we will be stuck with the current compromise and may lose our case completely, as the international strait interpretation does have a legal basis.

As in other dimensions of our relations with the Americans, they have interests against which it is futile to directly smash. We must find a way to dovetail with them while advancing our own interests.

We may not like it, but this is the game of a smaller ally in a tight trans-boundary relationship with a global hyper power.

We do not want to prevent the use of the Northwest Passage; we want to have control over its use. Fortunately, there is increasing interest in certain quarters of Washington for us to have that control.

But to exercise control over the use of the Passage we have to be more present in the Arctic, which ironically strengthens our position in Washington. We need more information and enforcement capacity — what are described as "the necessary control measures" — such as year-round ice breaker capability (which we currently do not have), sonar systems at the entrances to the Passage, pollution prevention and control equipment, and sufficient sea and land services for safe passage.[8]

There is no point in going head to head with the Americans within the paradigm of whether the Passage is an international strait or internal Canadian waters. It is a battle we will not win. It is much better that we work with the Americans at this propitious juncture and pursue this opportunity to find a compromise; one that gives us control, yet without the elusive satisfaction of the Passage being accepted as internal Canadian waters.[9]

As a student and teacher of Canadian-American relations I have always been amazed that we work in so many areas with the Americans, though not seemingly when it comes to the Arctic. Though that is something of an illusion, through NORAD we operate thirty-three warning stations with the Americans.

There is also the fiction that we don't know when U.S. submarines pass through the Canadian Arctic while our militaries operate together seamlessly. We know when a U.S. submarine leaves San Diego via the Canadian Arctic for a refit in Virginia, yet when the sub pops through the polar ice there is indignation in the Canadian press.

As we saw in the chapter on water we have a good neighbour's policy in the form of the Boundary Waters Treaty and the International Joint Commission. We co-manage the St. Lawrence

Seaway. It seems very likely we can find a better, less opaque way of working and cooperating with the Americans in the Arctic.

It is somewhat understandable, though, that we are suspicious of the U.S. in the Arctic. In our minds the issues are about sovereignty. We know from history that when Canadian and U.S. sovereign interests collide, we don't lose the cake but we lose the icing. One has only to go along our border to see that when there have been disagreements bits of icing have gone to the U.S. The most dramatic example concerns Alaska, which in the public imagination is in the north. There is a sense, and correctly so, that in the settlement of that boundary we got pushed around.

There were a handful of contentions in that dispute, but the really significant one was we came away without a port along the length of the panhandle. Theodore Roosevelt, the American president at the time of the agreement in 1903, was determined there be no Canadian port. As a result the border is 16.09 kilometres (10 miles) inland from the high-tide line.

Given the treaty inherited from the Russians our case was arguably weak. And, when you negotiate with a big, bold power, the goal is to keep the cake and accept that the U.S. is going to expect a good bit of icing — in this case about seven hundred kilometres of contiguous sovereignty along the Alaska Panhandle, leaving a huge area of British Columbia land-locked.

Let's apply this cake and icing principle to the Northwest Passage. In hindsight we realize we could have achieved a better deal on the Panhandle earlier with Roosevelt's predecessor, William McKinley, who was assassinated in 1901. The new president was more bellicose and the mood of the United States had changed.

Let us not make the same mistake now by waiting for a better moment to find a solution when the conjuncture might be less favourable. Our cake on the issue of the Passage is effective control and management. Beyond that the U.S. is not going to give up its global interests concerning free passage through international straits.

When we have a perceptibly weak case with the U.S. we are likely to lose, which could happen if we force the issue of the Passage as internal waters.

I am by inclination a pluralist and idealist who believes that all kinds of actors can come together in the international system to find enlightened solutions. But I am enough of realist to understand that the international system is also structured by nation states, and that in their clash of interests, the *realpolitik* dictum of "might is right" is not without basis. It is unwise, and unnecessary, to challenge the Americans bluntly in the international system with little hope of success.

I am not ideological about working with the Americans. Sometimes it makes sense to collaborate with them and other times to go it alone. The headlines in the spring of 2008 were captured by the story of a Canadian satellite, Radarsat-2, that provides images that help monitor our Arctic. The satellite's Canadian owners wanted to sell it to an American company. The government decided not to allow the sale, worried that we would lose access to the data.

The Radarsat-2 story reminds me of the Avro Arrow, a marvel of Canadian know-how that was cancelled. Both projects involved expensive cutting-edge Canadian technology paid for by taxpayers. They both involved cooperation and competition with the U.S. government. Their producers wanted contracts from the Americans to make them more economically viable.

The possible sale of the satellite and the earlier cancellation of the Avro Arrow solicited a strong reaction from Canadians, demonstrating that we desire to be an independent force in the world with our own sophisticated technologies.

Both point out the bind of being at times alone, with a lack of critical mass. Countries in Europe have dealt with this challenge by coming together to build things like the Airbus. The Avro Arrow was vastly out of proportion to our capacity. Luckily, Radarsat-2, though expensive, was not and continues to give us invaluable information; information that, in fact, reassures the U.S. we are serious about our northern border. Indeed, both our southern and northern borders need to be secure for the benefit of both Canada and the United States.[10]

The management of a secure North America includes the Arctic, and part of the reason a Canadian administered regime in the Passage is so promising is that the Americans don't see themselves as an Arctic nation, but as an Alaskan nation. If Canada is able to project capacity into the Arctic — there is some doubt as to whether we have the will and resources to build the necessary icebreakers — we can take the management of the Passage out of a paradigm of confrontation and put it into one of cooperation.

If elements within George W. Bush's Washington saw it this way, imagine what we might achieve with a much more multilaterally inclined President Obama.

I hope my treatment of this dimension of our relationship — in contrast with my conclusions about energy — confound those who strive to label analysis as left-nationalist or right-continentalist. Across the range of venues in our dance with the U.S. we can make decisions based not on these ideologies, but upon our national interests.

12
Manifest Destiny and Quebec

Much of the history of North America is a weave of relations between what were once French colonists and two types of British colonists — Loyalists and American patriots. For more than fifteen years, from 1760 to 1776, these groups lived under one sovereign authority and today find their expression in three political entities — Quebec, Canada, and the United States. The last and dominant of these has historically been somewhat animated by a policy of Manifest Destiny reflecting an appetite for expansion.

In high school history books, a number of maps illustrate the various stages of North American political development. Are we so temporal centric as to think that new maps will not be added? Relations between Canada and Quebec, and between Canada and the United States, are so central to the definition of Canada that any change in either relationship would significantly transform both our country and North America.

These relationships, while central to Canada, can pose a threat to it. Quebec has yet to sign the Constitution, and a formal compromise with the rest of Canada (ROC) not only appears unlikely, it seems implausible. Also, as we have seen, Canada is in the increasingly warm embrace of a single integrated bi-national economy, its fate tied more than ever to the world's only superpower.

The ramifications of North American economic integration are significant. The North American Free Trade Agreement includes a provision for renewable work permits that may be a harbinger of the free movement of people across borders. Policy collaboration may in the fullness of time lead to joint policy making that could increasingly come to resemble nascent political integration.

Initially, Canada came together in response to the challenges of its two central relationships — to bring Quebec in and keep America out. It now seems as if the dynamic may have reversed itself, with signs pointing to integration with the United States and, episodically, to disintegration with Quebec. There are, for our purposes, three pieces in the North American puzzle — Canada, the United States, and Quebec — and their relationships can be organized in different ways.

Integration with the U.S. continues, with an undetermined end point. Disintegration of Canada after the departure of Quebec is apt to compound this process. The ROC is not likely to be a very cohesive entity, and integration in varying degrees and speeds by its parts into the American colossus seems possible.

During the late 1980s and early 1990s, Canada unsuccessfully attempted to stabilize its relationship with Quebec by seeking a constitutional compromise. This failure prompted observers to consider the ramifications for the three pieces of the North American puzzle. A consensus emerged that the ROC would be an unsteady political edifice. In America, Canadian watchers began to wonder what this and growing economic integration might mean for the U.S.

It is natural and healthy for the Americans to enter into such reflections. There is an American tradition of expansionism, often described as Manifest Destiny, of wanting to possess all of North America. Is this tendency evident today? It can be argued that in the current climate of continental economic integration and free trade, and of globalization more generally, that it is possible to benefit from a territory without physically controlling it. Perhaps much of the logic of Manifest Destiny has passed.

However, Manifest Destiny also involves the belief that the U.S. is a chosen land that had been allotted all of North America by God. In this sense there is a current in American thinking that feels a God-given obligation and duty to share the benefits of its system throughout the continent and the world.

American restiveness with European influence in North America began when the U.S. emerged as a separate entity from the British Empire. Some early presidents felt the U.S. ought to have "natural dominion in North America." As American historian Gordon T. Stewart writes:

> American expansion was deemed to be in harmony with nature and geography; British and Canadian expansion was viewed as artificially instigated by imperial designs to check American growth. This view of matters, formed in the early national period, remained a basic element of the American mind-set.[1]

This "basic element of the American mind-set" finds its expression in a number of instances. On July 1, 1867, no congratulatory message came from Washington, but rather the announcement of the impending purchase of Alaska. During the 1870s, President Ulysses Grant described Canada as "unnatural," and President Rutherford Hayes wrote that "the annexation of Canada is our manifest destiny." In 1903 a settlement was reached in the Alaska boundary dispute, but the position of President Theodore Roosevelt had been so bellicose as to leave his Canadian counterpart Wilfrid Laurier bitter long into his retirement. And, finally, at the time of the proposed 1911 reciprocity agreement between Canada and the United States, a number of intemperate statements by American politicians contributed to the failure of the agreement to win support in Canada. A U.S. Senator declared that "Canadian annexation is the logical conclusion of reciprocity with Canada;" the Speaker of the House said, "We are preparing to annex Canada;" and, perhaps most famously, the House Democratic leader announced that he "looked forward to the time when the American flag will fly over every square foot of British North America up to the North Pole."

Though certainly not the dominant theme, it would seem plausible that at least some thin threads of Manifest Destiny and the related Monroe Doctrine against foreign influence in the Americas might be found in contemporary American reflections on the future of Canada. "Contemporary" is taken to mean since the mid-1960s; characterized initially by the nascent Quebec separatist movement within the context of its Quiet Revolution, and growing economic integration as embodied in the Canada-U.S. Auto Pact.

North America is becoming more economically integrated, and this is happening regardless of any annexationist tendencies in the U.S., or whether Quebec separates and the ROC disintegrates. As Canadian historian Jack Granatstein and others point out, Canada has been petitioning the U.S. for free trade since 1849.[2] Even Sir John A. Macdonald's famous National Policy was forced upon him by the rejection of Free Trade by a U.S. Senate still inflamed by British policy during the recent American Civil War. In 1886, 44 percent of Canadian exports went to the U.S., and in 1982 it was 68 percent. The record was in 2002 when 85 percent of Canadian exports went to the U.S.

The U.S. is a huge cultural and economic engine, a force in and on the world, and no country is more integrated with it or feels its impact and the weight of its policies as much as Canada. The prospect of emergent political convergence, if not indeed absorption, would likely only be quickened by Quebec separation and possible ROC disintegration.

The future of Canada is so intricately bound in its relationships with Quebec and with America, that in examining the U.S.

literature for hints of Manifest Destiny, it is difficult to separate American reflections based on Quebec separation and ROC disintegration from Canadian economic integration with the U.S.

This chapter is inspired by an article written by American academic Charles Doran in *Foreign Affairs* entitled, "Will Canada Unravel?" In this article, Doran urges the U.S. government to consider the consequences of ROC disintegration after Quebec's departure. He speculates that Washington would increasingly have to "Take on the jobs of peacemaker, adjudicator, rule-maker, and police officer."[3] While provocative and suggestive of an aggressive American position, closer examination shows that the article is not bristling with examples of Manifest Destiny. As Doran said when I interviewed him, "A Canadian can say it, and it's not even noticed. An American says it, and it's a crisis."[4] Indeed, once Canadians get beyond the emotional impact of Doran's observations, there is some basis for them. The article seems to find its premise in a book by journalist Lansing Lamont, as both works discuss the implications for the U.S. of what they call the worst case situation after the departure of Quebec. Evidence of Manifest Destiny is readily found in Lamont's book and to a lesser degree in another by policy analyst Jonathan Lemco. Significant though subtle evidence is also found, as we shall see, in a formerly secret U.S. State Department document.[5]

Doran writes, "Some analysts assume Canada is a cornucopia of minerals and raw materials that would suddenly open up, to U.S. advantage. Others believe that large new strategic benefits would flow to the U.S., for example, from adhesion of a coastal province."[6] Doran adds, "But each of these expectations is likely to disappoint."

Lemco writes: "Some provinces, especially BC, Alberta, and Ontario, might be particularly attractive to U.S. annexationists. Presumably, the U.S. would then enjoy an economic boom and be better able to compete with its economic rivals." And, "Latter-day Manifest Destiny is attractive to many Americans because of the goodwill they feel towards Canada and the vast storehouse of natural resources in Canada that would be most welcome additions to U.S. industrial strength."[7]

Lamont, who examines the worst case scenario after Quebec separation involving ROC disintegration, writes:

> The portents of America's absorption of Canada had been there right along. British military power and Confederation had blunted the thrust of 'manifest destiny.' Former U.S. Undersecretary of State, George Ball, had figured it right when he wrote in 1968 that Canada was fighting 'a rearguard action against the inevitable,' and that sooner or later Canada-American free trade would impel the integration of the two nations' economies. [This] would require an ever greater degree of 'political cohesion,' diplomatic puff for the U.S. absorption of Canada.[8]

He goes on to write:

> Just as U.S. authorities would prepare to slam the door on the provinces' requests for statehood, however, a second opinion might land on the President's desk. It would offer an assessment of Canada's natural resources in terms of America's benefit. The memo would start from the premise that Canada is sitting on the world's third richest mineral trove, with the third largest forest area, and one quarter of the planet's fresh surface water. It is not inconceivable that, having digested the memorandum, the President would

accede to requests from Alberta and BC to be admitted as states, Manitoba and Saskatchewan might be placed on associate status.[9]

Prominent American newspaper columnists such as William Safire, Peter Brimelow, and Pat Buchanan have also written that Quebec secession and its ramifications would be in the interest of the U.S., and that America might gain by swallowing parts of a divided Canada.[10]

Much more subtle is the comment by the careful U.S. academic Joseph Jockel, who writes: "To be sure, should the day ever come when parts of Canada applied for admission to the Union, it would be very difficult to refuse them entry."[11] But we are left to speculate as to why "it would be very difficult." This guarded style is found in the once secret American State Department report, "The Quebec Situation: Outlook and Implications." In considering the disintegration of Canada, the report states, "The U.S. would be faced with new opportunities" that could be "positive," and that, "Nevertheless, the present situation also is not to our benefit."[12] Of interest in the last phrase are the words "nevertheless" and "also," which seem to infer that while the prospect of Canadian disintegration poses problems "nevertheless" it could "also" be of benefit to the U.S.

Canadian prime ministers have certainly seen the benefits to the U.S. if it annexed Canada. Sir John A. Macdonald once said, "Every American statesman covets Canada." In the mid-1940s, Mackenzie King was moved to say, "The long-range plan of the Americans is to control the continent, to turn Canada into a part of the U.S." And, upon the election in 1976 of the Parti Québécois, Pierre Trudeau is reported to have been "Anxious and concerned as to whether the Americans would seize the PQ victory as an opportunity to redraw the boundaries of North America."

There are also echoes of the Monroe Doctrine among some of today's political analysts. In 1823, President James Monroe made a statement which bears his name in which he opposed the influence of European powers in the Americas. Doran writes that "Continuing fragmentation potentially involves powers outside North America in special treaties and coalitions."[13] And a colleague Joseph Jockel writes:

> Clearly, a major goal of a sovereign Quebec's foreign policy would be to pursue close ties with other francophone states, especially France, and to play a major role as a sovereign member in the Francophonie. Thanks to Paris-Quebec ties, it is easy to conjure up images of Quebec, as the 'EC's Trojan horse' in economic discussions. To be sure, there will be issues on which Quebec will agree with the Europeans.[14]

North America, for the sake of these ruminations, is built upon the relationships of three political units. Sufficiently alter the nature of these relations and the political structure of North America is also changed. The separation of Quebec from Canada is such a change, as is the potential integration of the ROC into the United States. All of this would take place against a backdrop of growing continental integration led by economic factors, and through more recent collaboration against terrorism.

In considering the future of North America, the attitude of the U.S., the dominant piece of the puzzle, is significant. Are America's reflections upon the future of North America still informed by Manifest Destiny, as they once so clearly were? Contemporary U.S. literature indicates, not surprisingly, that there are some threads of annexationist sentiment. But the U.S., and the position of the U.S. in the world, are now so different than they were at the time of Manifest Destiny's hey-day that such inclinations are tempered by other more pressing and immediate considerations.

Manifest Destiny is a historical vestige and can perhaps still be seen as an element in a more complex constellation of American concerns and interests. But its real power is not in the American mind, but in the Canadian mind, contributing to our sense of vulnerability and fear of the U.S. It is largely in this way that it continues to have significance.

Part IV
Conclusion

13

Beyond Our Shared Continent: Canada in the World

If there are best practices for Canada's continental engagement with the U.S., there are also best practices for Canada's role in the world. Chief among them is that we succeed when we do not succumb to believing Canada's role comes down to two options — that we must either follow or reject the U.S.

Our contrasting ideological predispositions on how to engage the Americans dramatically colour and can also get in the way when we go into the wider world.

The international system is like the gears of a watch. To make the most effective contribution, Canada must understand and take its place within the timepiece of international diplomacy. This is not the same as taking the role of junior partner to the U.S.

We make our maximum contribution to the world by capitalizing on our comparative advantage. Former president Bill Clinton described this well, when he told me in an interview after leaving office that: "Canada is well-trusted for a Western nation. You can use that, as you have for example in Haiti. Canada could also make a real impact in the Darfur region of Sudan, as you are able to participate there without the resentments of the U.S." He added, "Appreciate the value of your unique contribution as the basis for Canadian engagement in the world."[1]

We have nothing to add to the U.S. in terms of brute force. This is a capacity largely unique to the U.S. Our capacities and how we fit into the international system gives us different choices.

Why would we want to attempt to mimic the contribution of the U.S.? To do so would only undermine the contribution we can make within the international community.

We must remember that Canada and the U.S. share many of the same values. Where we diverge dramatically, where we do not share, and cannot share, is a common understanding of our roles in the international community. The U.S. is a massive country in wealth, capacity, size, and population. Canada is not, and thus lives far more the experience of the rest of the world. So Canada is inclined to advise the Americans, and our views are often similar to, and perhaps reinforce, orientations that compete within the American policy-making community.

We make our best contribution when we do what the Americans largely cannot do, or do less adroitly. When we have more facility in the international system we are more valuable. This gives us more influence in Washington and with other countries. And so there is a virtuous circle: the U.S. places more value upon us, and other countries are in turn more interested in us.

We can be a needed gear within the clock of international diplomacy.[2] That is how we find our greatest relevance and realize opportunity for the world and its central power.

Canada's military engagement in Kandahar demands all of our capacity, does not differentiate us from the Americans, and dulls our currency. In Haiti we make an immediate and unique impact. We would be in a position to take similar leadership in Sudan if we were not over-extended in Afghanistan.

Our contributions to building the U.N. and NATO, the U.N.'s Universal Declaration of Human Rights, the Colombo Development Plan, and more recently the Convention on Land Mines and the International Criminal Court — two initiatives not backed by the U.S. — all support the principles of multilateralism: the rule of law and international stability.

Our military contribution had been characterized by peacekeeping, but today circumstances have changed and we are involved in more missions of a peacemaking nature. We should not be confused by this transition. While such missions need to be on a sensible scale they are normally consistent with our national identity and traditions as practical advocates for peace.

We must also continue to support peace through peace building — creating the conditions for peace through prosperity. We must come closer to realizing our stated goal of 0.7 percent of GDP going to international development assistance. Africa — with 800 million people and 1 percent of world trade — should be an ongoing focus for our efforts.

How we do international relations is a model for the world, as many countries face similar considerations. When we get it right, we contribute to the template of the international system.

We do not need to be surrogates for the U.S. or be locked into suspicion and rejection of the U.S. Neither approach leads to the full contribution Canada can make in the world.

In 1956 Canada advanced a peacekeeping force as a way of resolving the Suez Crisis. When Britain and France took control of the Suez Canal the U.S. was opposed and NATO was in jeopardy. Within that context, Canada led the world with an independent foreign policy.

One of the problems our peacekeepers faced was they arrived with the Red Ensign on their shoulders. We were misunderstood as agents of a less-trusted power. This is one of the reasons we adopted our own distinct national flag. Let us heed this lesson and not repeat it by having the maple leaf misunderstood as the stars and stripes.

Before concluding this chapter, let's develop a few of the points made above and consider some other elements.

China Card

There were the beginnings of a discussion about our place in the world during the most recent softwood lumber dispute with the U.S. During the 1988 election, Canadians voted to support free trade with the Americans because they agreed to create and respect the decisions of a dispute settlement panel. In the recent softwood dispute, the U.S. was ignoring the panel's ruling in favour of the Canadian position, so in 2006 the prime minister at the time, Paul Martin, played a new card — China.

The Middle Kingdom is attracting a lot of attention with its 1.3 billion inhabitants and its almost 10 percent-per-year economic growth rate. Mr. Martin suggested Canada might encourage the construction of a proposed pipeline to the B.C. coast for export of oil to China; oil that would otherwise have gone to the U.S.

China represents, perhaps for the first time, a realistic possibility of diversifying our trade. Something Prime Ministers Diefenbaker and Trudeau also attempted in response to spats with the Americans: Diefenbaker by increasing trade with the Commonwealth and Trudeau with his Third Option to Europe.

While China is useful in our discussions with the Americans, it is not a trump card.

Iraq, Ballistic Missile Defence, and Afghanistan

At first glance Iraq, Ballistic Missile Defence (BMD), and Afghanistan appear unrelated. Yet they are so bound together, they are almost of a piece; a dramatic example of how we wilfully misunderstand both our relationship with the U.S. and how the American system of government works.

We hold a perverse coin of fear which we flip between defiance and a desire to please the imperial centre. A coin with no winning side. We have seen this so often within North America and you see it quickly and powerfully in our foreign policy beyond North America. We make major decisions based on our preoccupation with and misunderstanding of Washington. We think they are paying attention and they are not. We think they act with one voice, responding as a unified coercive, cohesive force when they do not. These are observations that say more about us than about the U.S.

Here's the chain of events from Iraq through Ballistic Missile Defence that led to the nature and extent of our current involvement in Afghanistan.

The Americans spend almost as much on BMD each year as we do on all of our military – about $17 billion. The purpose of BMD is to bring down missiles that may someday be fired by rogue states, such as North Korea and Iran, before they reach the U.S.

The Americans wanted us to base a radar site with interceptor missiles on the east coast in defence against missiles attacks from the Middle East. Under Paul Martin, Canada declined to directly participate in BMD on the basis that we did not want to support the weaponization of space. But we met American basic requirements by agreeing to include sharing of missile-launch warning information through NORAD.

Earlier, Prime Minister Chrétien had said "no" to direct participation in the war in Iraq. But we have been more active in the "coalition of the willing" through things such as routine secondment of our military than many of the other countries which officially joined.

Despite having quietly met the basic requirements of cooperation with the U.S. in both Iraq and BMD, Ottawa felt strongly that Canada had got too far offside with the Americans and needed to make amends.

This argument is wonderfully developed by Janice Stein and my friend Eugene Lang in their book *The Unexpected War: Canada in Kandahar.* Lang was chief of staff to two defence ministers during the Chrétien-Martin period. From first-hand experience of how the process worked, he writes: "Despite the evidence that the Canada-U.S. relationship had suffered little or no damage Ottawa felt a sense of urgency to do something to offset the negative consequences of what they feared."[3]

I will return to this notion of fear in the conclusion and how it animates a colonial mindset. It is a fear that instills an impulse to defy or to please; that makes it hard for us to rationally engage the U.S.

The something we did to "offset the [imagined] negative consequences" of not signing on to BMD and the war in Iraq was our robust participation in Afghanistan.

As Stein and Lang so effectively recount, we got into Afghanistan as a dimension of our relationship with the U.S. — and our misunderstanding of that relationship. In my view, we negotiated against ourselves, constructing a false loyalty test. As a result, well over one hundred Canadians have died in Afghanistan to date.

This has been unnecessary. We can go into the wider world with values genuinely similar to the U.S. without fundamentally being an American spear carrier. We make a bigger, more unique contribution to the clockwork of the international system, in part, by being more helpful to the U.S., by imagining ourselves less fully as a junior partner.

14

In the Groove: From Fear to Opportunity

A hazard with this project was having it descend into our perennial discussion of "What it is to be Canadian." Yet that is an element in what we are talking about. More than a lingering colonial mentality is impeding us from clearly understanding our options with the U.S. Not immune to such habits, this book is also an attempt to understand my identity as a Canadian.

So maybe it is not such a bad thing to step back and say, "Okay, we've been putting this off long enough, let's look for a moment at who we are in terms of people, identity, and values."

In the chapter on the Avro Arrow, the question of who we are as a people looms large in understanding the significance of that aircraft and its cancellation. It combines threads of our identity, values, and national psyche and makes them vibrate.

We are a separate, different country that is also hugely contextualized by our neighbour. We share things in common and have divergences. We may seem to be Minnesota with Mounties. Are we more than unarmed Americans with health insurance?

We share similar values with about 45 million Americans. While that is 12 million more Americans than Canadians, it is still only about 15 percent of the American population. Moreover, these shared values have a regional basis so there is contiguity across the border.[1]

There is a reason we can finish each other's sentences, and why first generation Canadians blend directly into being Americans while for others this happens in the second generation.

Part of the explanation is the long history of unimpeded movement of people back and forth across the border. Millions have done so since the Loyalists came to British North America after what some describe as the first American Civil War.

From 1850 to 1900, 1.5 million Canadians left for the U.S., which meant that one in five native-born Canadians in 1900 lived in the U.S.[2] Today the Canadian-born population in Los Angeles and New York City is equivalent to a large Canadian city. One and a half million Canadians are in Florida every February, which is about 5 percent of our population.

Part of the challenge for Canada has been to write our own story. American Manifest Destiny has been significant historically. "God bless America" is pretty similar to "God blessed America," and we have been offered membership in the blessed republic. One section in the failed first constitution of the U.S., the Articles of Confederation, reads "Canada shall be admitted into and entitled to all the advantages of the union."

We having been saying "No thank you" for some time now, including in 1867 when one of our fathers of confederation, George-Étienne Cartier, wrote: "The matter resolved itself into this, either we must obtain British North American Confederation or be absorbed into the American Confederation."

The Canadian story, like the American, is a North American one. So the potential to think of ourselves as North Americans is there. And as we have seen, there are those from both the continentalist right and nationalist left who would have us think about a North American Community. They always include Mexico in the equation, as we have discussed, lulling us into thinking the idea isn't primarily about a joint community with the U.S.

There is a tendency to see North America as a single place when it comes not only to economics but also to security and post-9/11 initiatives to "zip-lock" the continent from external threats. Measures to secure North America are also thickening the border, so for all the impetus of integration there is also at the moment some disintegrative momentum.

People construct identities in part as acts of imagination. Our identity is a kind of home in which we live. From identity and values come premises, prescriptions, and outcomes.

At this, as in all junctures of our national life, we must be careful about going down a North American Community path. The mixing and merging of peoples is the story of human existence. A free trade agreement and perhaps, some day, a customs union is one thing, but the completely free movement of labour across our border will ultimately see the merging of our two countries.

We must be mindful to guard against this. There is at the moment a thin edge of the wedge — NAFTA temporary work visas. In 1996 there were almost twenty-seven thousand of these issued to Canadians to work in the U.S. By 2007, almost 165,000 Canadians were working in the U.S. as temporary workers.[3] An underlying question of this trend is: "If good fences make good neighbours, what do no fences make?"

We have a close and important affinity with our North American partners, but we must be wary. The wind of blending into the U.S. blows gently and constantly. Some have suggested a really good storm could turn the pivot of Canadian identity; like flipping a board in the wind.

To facilitate deeper integration with the U.S., Canadian identity has to be softened up. Some on the continentalist right do this by promoting the idea of a North American Community.[4] Others suggest a terrorist attack on Canada could be the blast blowing us into closer identification and subsequent further integration with the U.S.[5]

As John Holmes, a former diplomat and scholar of Canada's international affairs, writes in *Life with Uncle: The Canadian-American Relationship*:

Great caution has [to be] exercised over schemes which prescribe a North American entity because the facts of population and resources are such that the life we Canadians have built for ourselves over three centuries would soon be drained out of us.[6]

Colonial Mentality

Why do we wilfully ignore how the American system of government and decision making works? If we eased our determined construal of our interests as contingent upon approval from an amorphous U.S. we could allow ourselves to make different decisions.

We fixate on whether our position will bother the U.S. without rationally considering their response; ascribing to "the Americans" implausible retributions and ideas they have never thought of.

A plausible explanation for this phenomenon is the problem of a colonial mentality. It speaks to our identity being incomplete, and that we identify with another larger country instead of our own, and certainly in addition to our own.

When considering the demise of the Avro Arrow, the engineers said, "We'd come back and do good quality engineering if the right thing came along." Almost forty years later, Dan Aykroyd, the star in the documentary that depicts the end of the Avro Arrow and who lives and works in Los Angeles, was asked what would bring him back to Canada. Perhaps unwittingly, he echoed the engineers when he replied, "I would come back to do good quality historical drama if the right thing came along."[7]

Our relationship with this much more powerful country can lead to and reinforce feelings of inferiority. Only 2 percent of the movies we watch in English are Canadian. On English television we are the only OECD country that doesn't have a home-grown drama among its ten most popular television programs.

This is the type of thing that perhaps leads to the results of a recent poll showing that while the world loves Canada, Canadians doubt their worth.[8]

It's difficult to marshal empirical evidence to scientifically measure how colonial habits work. Writer Lawrence Martin describes the phenomenon and its hopeful trajectory this way: "For a long time, Canada's colonial heritage fed its dependency mentality. But the country is older, more populated, more confident. It has come of age, as the cliché has it, and with maturity, the sense of self-doubt and subordination has diminished."[9]

As the leading essayist and public intellectual John Ralston Saul writes, for some there is a "sense that reality is not here, but elsewhere, in another culture, another market, as part of another elite."[10]

This colonial mentality has some of us wanting to go into the world as America's best friend. This is much more a need we feel than a request being made of us. This mentality seems to lead to wild swings between superiority and inferiority that fuel, and manifest in, our left-nationalists and right-continentalists.

It's as if we have a victim mentality in our relationship with the Americans and we do not recognize our own strength. If we need the Americans they also need us. Canada is the largest export market for thirty-seven of the fifty U.S. states. The value of our two-way trading relationship is about $2 billion dollars a day. The value of U.S. vehicle exports to Canada is larger than its total exports to any European country. Total U.S. exports to Canada are larger than exports to Mexico and Japan combined. The U.S. is highly dependent on foreign energy, and we supply them with more energy than any other country.[11] All of this speaks to the power we have in our relationship with the U.S. We are much less victim than we are partner.

While I argue that it is not anti-American to be pro-Canadian, there is solid ground for the assessment that there is a strong anti-American streak in Canadian life. And the reason for this is our colonial mentality; a lack of maturity that has us reacting to the U.S. like petulant teenagers.

Politicians play on this. During the 2005 election, Prime Minister Paul Martin accused his opponent of "harbouring 'American-style' intentions," as if Stephen Harper was harbouring a fugitive. To describe something as American-style is often an all-purpose insult that cuts off debate.

Going back to elections in the nineteenth century, proposals for closer relations with the U.S. have been successfully challenged using terms such as "veiled treason."

Our huge intake of new Canadians may contribute to overcoming pre-existing approaches and attitudes. For years we have been the first or second largest recipient of immigrants per capita — some 175,000 to 225,000 per year. Many of these new Canadians are not prisoners of our old mindsets. They may encourage us toward enlightened global engagement and a more mature understanding of the nature of our relationship with our neighbour.

We suffer from a transcendent fear. Fear of letting the Americans buy the Arrows for us in the late 1950s, fear of working with them in the Arctic now, fear in selling them an unlimited amount of oil and natural gas, fear to sell them water, fear of engaging them alone and engaging them ineffectually with Mexico, fear of the imagined consequences of our tacit but not fulsome support in Iraq and on BMD, a fear whose embrace has lead us to our current role in Afghanistan. Fear of America's Manifest Destiny to the continent.

I didn't set out thinking about fear. Though I understand now my motivation for this project involved fear; fear that we were being drawn into the American maw. I was fearful because of my uncertain Canadian identity: relatives kept being drawn into the U.S., and the influence of America in our lives can often be overwhelming. In trying to understand our neighbour I've been trying to understand ourselves, myself. This is in part a consideration of community and of imagined community.

We stand on the cusp, on the threshold of understanding our fear of and longing for the U.S. — of rather than laying down ideological creeds lifting up Canadian needs.

In North America, and as we have seen in the wider world, let's stop being preoccupied with imagining what the U.S. wants or doesn't want of us.

The first step in realization is, of course, imagining. Let us imagine a new project, one free of a colonial mindset and the overarching and underpinning fear that surrounds it.

To do this we must change the way we manage our relationship with the U.S. We must realize we are engaging a vast, self-absorbed, and segmented neighbour. It is a country that doesn't think about Canada. And when it does, its power and interests are diffused.

We must appreciate that the U.S. also needs Canada, and that in the relationship Canada is much more than a mouse in bed with an elephant.

We need to be a Canada that doesn't sell all the oil and natural gas to the Americans that we possibly can but not a drop of water; a Canada that seizes the moment for a regulatory regime in the Arctic by seeing the U.S. as an ally; and a Canada that understands that notions of American Manifest Destiny have their real power not in the American, but in the Canadian mind.

The handling of our possible participation in the American-led invasion of Iraq is a good example of how the continentalist right and the nationalist left faced a challenge in our relationship with the U.S. The former wanted us go to Iraq to fight with the Americans and the latter said "No," but did so with such anger as to undermine our relationship.

The U.S. was not overly concerned whether we went or not. What they did not like, and what diminished our relationship, was that we said "No" with such a string of insults.

Neither of these approaches was in our interest. Both reflect a mindset that has us swing between truculence and a desire to please.

Our calling is to go into the wider world, not as a junior partner of the U.S., but realizing our more unique potential to contribute within the clockwork of the international system.

It's not the U.S. that is the problem; it's how *we* think about the U.S. Our relationship isn't so much about them as it is about us.

Big Steps, No Thank You

We are hooked and hinged with each other in constant cooperation and clash. We should enter into agreements with the Americans to reduce conflict, not in the first instance to bring us closer together.

And yet we are bombarded by the silver bullets of efficient solutions, of big steps and grand bargains.

We suffer under the largely unchallenged misunderstanding that free trade with the Americans "undoubtedly made us wealthier." Instead, the facts are that before free trade hardly any tariffs existed. As well, the rate of increase in trade with the Americans has been largely constant both before and after free trade. And the increase in trade that did take place in the 1990s was over 90 percent due to the cheap Canadian dollar and the robust American economy.[12]

The biggest impact of NAFTA was psychologically to make us feel more closely associated with the U.S., and sadly to lock in the export of what is now well over half of our natural gas and oil production while our reserves of natural gas and conventional oil are declining.

Whenever there is a challenge in our relationship there are calls for closer relations with the U.S. During the recession of 2009, as Canada grew concerned about Buy-American laws, comments began to re-emerge advocating a new solution — to engage the Americans more fully, tied to the safeguard of doing so with Mexico. A *Globe and Mail* editorial calling for deeper free trade concludes with:

> Given the large disproportion between the U.S. and Canada, the tri-lateral approach — including Mexico — offers a way forward that Canadians need to think about seriously.[13]

Yet it is as true now as when John Holmes wrote almost thirty years ago:

> An illusion that goads us is that there is a solution. Some understanding that would end all conflict, settle disputes or perhaps do away with them altogether.[14]

Seeing every disagreement with the Americans as a problem and looking for a grand solution is like carrying a hammer when everything looks like a nail. Holmes also wrote:

> The Canadian nation is constantly threatened by the ruthless drive towards the most efficient organization of this continent, but the juggernaut is Canadian as well as American in its mindless propulsion.[15]

This "ruthless drive towards the most efficient organization of this continent" has led us to see Canadian oil and natural gas production in terms of North American energy security; which is to say in terms of U.S. needs and Canadian profits.

Much of the impetus in the history of the western hemisphere is about making money. That's why Walter Raleigh came to North America and it is why Alexander Mackenzie was the first European to cross it. The motivation, in the first instance, was not nation-building — it was the pursuit of riches.

An unbridled logic of money making leads us to continental integration, to one North America. It is part of what fuels Holmes's observation that "continentalism is a force of nature."

A danger in our debate is that influential economists on the continentalist right extrapolate from a narrow base of expertise — without a countervailing or competing logic — to make far-reaching prescriptions.

A leitmotif of Canadian life is said to be survival — against the elements and with such a dispersed population faced with the U.S. When, as the smaller power, we go to the Americans as the demander, it is essential that we figure out what we want.

Our relationship with the Americans can be overwhelming. For example, when the government does a review of our foreign relations, those with the U.S. are largely unexamined as they are so pervasively broad and deep.

To give a sense of the magnitude of just our trading relationship with the U.S., Canada sells more to Home Depot than it does to France.

Our economic relationship with the U.S. is huge, with about 80 percent of our exports going there. But that figure is often used to scare us into big solutions and further integration, while trade linkages among Canadian provinces remain twenty times as dense as those between Canadian provinces and U.S. states.[16]

Yet, we can get huge benefits from our relationship with the Americans. Think of the auto sector, where, through the Auto Pact, we build 20 percent of the vehicles produced in North

America, though our population is only 10 percent of the U.S. It's an example of what we did not do with the Avro Arrow. There was a possibility that went unexplored, that the Americans would have paid for the planes. In other words, we declined huge benefits that might have stayed in Canada.

Two Essential Steps

Raymond Chrétien, a former Canadian ambassador to the U.S., has said we face a big challenge to reap the benefits of the relationship while strengthening our values, beliefs, and institutions.[17]

And Lloyd Axworthy, a former minister of foreign affairs, has written that we must move beyond nationalist and continentalist stereotypes that replace analysis and obscure the search for new thinking.[18]

Doing the Continental meets the "challenge" and moves beyond the "stereotypes."

I am not a middle-of-the-road advocate for not taking a decision. The orientation and preoccupations of this book form a new and sensible basis for making decisions and taking steps towards doing our dance with the U.S. differently.

John Holmes has asked: "How do we manage and discipline continentalism as a force of nature that should never be encouraged?" It is not anti-American to lean against and shape the forces of integration. A constructive relationship with the U.S. is essential to achieving our basic national interests, not to please the United States but to promote ourselves.

How we engage the Americans and the future it affords is largely up to us, not them. The nub of the challenge is not the Americans but how we think about them.

Our relationship with the U.S. is one of our two big perennial concerns. The other is the rest of Canada's relationship with

Quebec. The Quebec issue seems dormant for the moment, but that could easily change,[19] as discussed in Chapter 12.

Some say it is unlikely that Canada would ever find its way into union with the U.S., and that the Canadian state will survive indefinitely because American conservatives would never condone or endorse the annexation of Canada's left-leaning population, which would tip the balance in the American political system decisively in favour of the Democrats.[20] Yet, I think that at the end of the day, the U.S. could absorb us as part of a natural process.

Change in our relationship with the Americans is inescapable and the more gradual and hidden the change the more decisive. We began, in part, as an American settlement, with the United Empire Loyalists coming to Canada after arguably the first American civil war. In the fullness of time, we seem to be becoming again less apart and what might be considered an accident of history could be repaired.

This possibility is why we must push back against the natural force of continentalism — which we embrace at our peril.

It can happen in pieces, as with the growing network of transborder pipelines that send ever increasing amounts of our declining natural gas and conventional oil reserves to the U.S., confirming ourselves as hewers of wood and drawers of oil.

So far as energy is concerned, Clayton Yeutter, the U.S. trade representative, was right when, in 1987, he said of the Canada-U.S. Free Trade Agreement: "We've signed a stunning new trade pact with Canada. The Canadians don't understand what they've signed. In 20 years, they will be sucked into the U.S. economy."[21]

The arrival of a new president in the White House presents new opportunities for our relationship with the United States. President Obama talks a lot about fear, and moving beyond fear to imagining new, better relationships within the U.S. and with the world.

It's an interesting coming together of a new president, his message, and what this book is humbly advancing — that we get into the groove of doing the continental by moving from fear to opportunity.

Final Refrain

The challenge to our relationship of 9/11 was pronounced and so the piling on of solutions was fast and furious; thirteen significant integrative proposals in the two years that followed.

While I've been fascinated by, and had a mind to write a book on, Canadian-American relations for a long time, that was the context when I started to seriously engage this project. It felt like Canada was in the strike zone. Would we hit the ball of integration with the U.S.? The stadium seemed to be built and the players ready and on the field. Everything seemed as if it was being set up for us to hit the ball out of the stadium and come closer to ending the game. Or even, as John Holmes says, "For Canadians [to realize what] has always seemed to be available, if all else failed, that final solution of continental union."[22]

That a political scientist would write a book that includes himself is understandable, as the idea that the writer is and should be detached from his work is often a fiction. It is often more honest as a social scientist to admit that one is part of his surroundings and that interrogation is also a personal journey within a larger community. That we are grounded in community is why a story that includes the individual more likely speaks to others. Such a book is of interest not only for its content apart from the writer, but also for what is a part of the writer.

I sought to understand Canada and Quebec by learning French in my twenties and doing a Ph.D. at the Université de Montréal. Writing this book is an attempt to understand that other great dimension of our collective life — the role and place of the U.S.

This is my response, after many years, to Bruce Goff's thought-provoking and irritating comment that Canada and the United States are "The same piece of real estate."

Appendix
Twelve Steps for Doing the Continental

----

1) There is no BIG solution in our relationship with the U.S.

2) Continentalism is a force of nature that we have to be wary of and tame for our national interests.

3) Our debate in Canada about how to engage the Americans is polarized and ideological. It has its basis in a lingering colonial mindset of over-arching and underpinning fear that has our policies vacillating between truculence and wanting to please the Americans.

4) Manifest Destiny has deep historical roots, but its real power today is not in the American but in the Canadian mind, contributing to our sense of vulnerability and fear of the U.S.

5) The U.S. is vast and preoccupied with domestic issues and international hot spots. Its system of government is divided and it rarely acts towards allies as a unified corporate force. The nature of our debate informs a wilful misunderstanding of how the U.S. and its system of government works to protect us from the retributions we imagine. We have much more freedom to act than we realize.

6) Our relationship is based on the massive, mutual self-interest and interdependence of *both* parties. America may

be an elephant, but it is in bed with a hippo or a muskox, not a mouse.

7) By placing Mexico centrally in our relations with the U.S., we are not achieving the benefits of multilateralism. We must resist the corrosive notion of a North American Community, in part presented as being "Okay" because it includes Mexico.

8) We have unnecessarily locked ourselves into exporting what is now much more than half of our production of natural gas and oil, as our reserves of natural gas and conventional oil are in serious decline. We have done this in part due to what seems, for the moment, to be intractable issues within our domestic politics.

9) While we export as much oil and natural gas as we possibly can, the mood is we must never export a drop of water to our neighbour, when, in fact, Canada has for decades diverted massive amounts of water to river systems in the U.S.

10) In the Arctic, controversy concerning Canadian jurisdiction over the Northwest Passage might best be resolved, not by seeing the Americans as the problem, but as the solution.

11) When we go beyond our shared continent, into the wider world, we are more effective and ironically more helpful to our leading ally when we imagine ourselves less fully as a junior partner.

12) It is not the U.S. that is the problem; it is how we think about the U.S. Our relationship is not so much about them as it is about us.

Further Reading

Chapter 2:
Avro Arrow: The World's Fastest Fighter Jet Runs Out of Fuel

A good introduction to the Avro Arrow is a DVD distributed by CBC Home Video called *The Arrow*, produced in 1997 — always in stock at the Canadian Museum of Aviation in Ottawa. The movie, which stars Dan Aykroyd, advances the mythology of the Arrow as Canada's promise denied. This is a useful video, as are the special features on the DVD.

There are specialized books on the Arrow that go into a lot of details. A good starting point is Greig Stewart, *Shutting Down the National Dream*, McGraw-Hill Ryerson, 1988. You can also find material within books: such as a chapter on the Arrow in Denis Smith's *Rogue Tory: The Life and Legend of John G. Diefenbaker*, Macfarlane Walter & Ross, 1995; and discussion in Jack Granatstein's *Canada 1957–67*, McClelland & Stewart, 1986.

Part II:
Continental Dance: Managing the Relationship

An interesting resource in which managing the relationship is discussed are the autobiographies of former Canadian ambassadors to Washington and other senior Canadian political figures. Amongst these you may want to look at: Lloyd Axworthy, *Navigating a New World: Canada's Global Future*, Toronto: Alfred A. Knopf, 2003; Eddie Goldenberg, *The Way It Works: Inside Ottawa*, Toronto: McClelland & Stewart, 2006; Allan Gotlieb, *The Washington Diaries*, Toronto: McClelland & Stewart, 2006; and Derek Burney, *Getting It Done: A Memoir*, Montreal: McGill-Queen's University Press, 2005.

Chapter 8:
What's Mexico Got to Do with It: Continental Counterweight or Deadweight?

Two sources — Jean Daudelin, "The Trilateral Mirage: A Tale of Two North Americas," Paper prepared for the Canadian Defence and Foreign Affairs Institute, June 2003; and Jimena Jimenez, "Trilateral Dysfunctions: Management Issues Related to the Creation of a North American Community," paper presented at the Canadian Political Science Association Annual Conference, May 30 to June 1, 2003 — make an important contribution to the orientation of this chapter.

Other useful readings include:

- Senate of Canada, "Mexico: Canada's Other NAFTA Partner." *Report of the Standing Senate Committee on Foreign Affairs* 3 (March 2004).
- Lloyd Axworthy. *Navigating a New World: Canada's Global Future*. Toronto: Alfred A. Knopf Canada, 2003.
- Anthony DePalma. *Here: A Biography of the New American Continent*. Toronto: HarperCollins, 2002.
- Rogelio Ramirez de la O. "Mexico: NAFTA and the Prospects for North American Integration." *The Border Papers, C.D. Howe Institute Commentary*, November 2002.

- Dwight Mason. "The Canada-United States Relationship: Is There a View from Washington?" *Commentary*, a publication of the Royal Canadian Military Institute, December 2005.

Chapter 9:
An Energy Superpower Without an Energy Strategy

Peter Tertzakian's *A Thousand Barrels a Second: The Coming Oil Break Point and the Challenges Facing an Energy Dependent World* (New York: McGraw-Hill, 2006) is a good introduction to the global energy context.

Hugh McCullum, "Fueling Fortress America, A Report on the Athabasca Tar Sands and U.S. Demands for Canada's Energy," (*Canadian Centre for Policy Alternatives*, March 2006) is one of the few documents from the nationalist left that addresses this issue.

Don Gillmor's "Shifting Sands" (*The Walrus*, April 2005) is a feature article dealing with the Alberta tar sands.

Monica Gattinger's "From Government to Governance in the Energy Sector: The States of the Canada-U.S. Energy Relationship," (*The American Review of Canadian Studies*, Summer 2005) is an academic treatment of the Canada-U.S. energy relationship and is a good and rare synthesis.

Chapter 10:
Not Watertight

The Canadian Institute of International Affairs' National Capital Branch's Study Group on Water Resources produced a useful overview, "The Transboundary Water Resources of Canada and the United States," in 2005, which can be found at *www.ciia.org/*

nawgroup.htm.

Tony Clark's "Turning on Canada's Tap?: Why We Need a Pan-Canadian Policy and Strategy Now on Bulk Water Exports to the U.S.," (A Polaris Institute Report in collaboration with the Canadian Centre for Policy Alternatives, Canadian Labour Congress, and the Sierra Club of Canada, April 2008) is a representative document of perspectives from the dedicated nationalist left.

Chris Wood, "Melting Point: How Global Warming Will Melt Our Glaciers, Empty the Great Lakes, Force Canada to Divert Rivers, Build Dams, and, Yes Sell Water to the United States," (*The Walrus*, October 2005) explores those issues and is a nice read.

A work that covers a range of water issues in Canada is *Eau Canada: The Future of Canada's Water*, edited by Karen Bakker and published by UBC Press in 2007. A particularly relevant chapter is by John B. Sprague, "Great Wet North? Canada's Myth of Water Abundance."

The work of the Program on Water Issues at the Munk Centre for International Studies at the University of Toronto is also of interest and can be found at *www.powi.ca*.

Chapter 11:
Defrosting Arctic Sovereignty

Studies of Canada and our situation in the Arctic are conducted by a handful of political scientists and law school professors. Three of the leading political scientists are Franklyn Griffiths, Rob Huebert, and Michael Byers, and amongst the leading lawyers are Donald McRae, Donat Pharand, and Suzanne Lalonde. Each of them has produced various articles and, in some cases, books.

A good way to find material on this subject is through articles in the *International Journal* and the series *Behind the Headlines*, both published by the Canadian International Council. In

Behind the Headlines I recommend "Arctic Sovereignty? What is at Stake?" by Donald McRae (64, no. 1, 2007) and the multi-authored "Canada's Arctic Interests and Responsibilities" (65, no. 4, 2008).

Chapter 12:
Manifest Destiny and Quebec

Charles Doran's article "Will Canada Unravel?" (*Foreign Affairs*, 75, no. 5, September/October 1996) is fascinating and was a prod for this chapter.

Some essential books on the topic are: Jean-François Lisée, *In the Eye of the Eagle* (Toronto: HarperCollins, 1990); Jonathan Lemco, *Turmoil in the Peaceable Kingdom: The Quebec Sovereignty Movement and Its Implications for Canada and the United States* (Toronto: University of Toronto Press, 1994); and Lansing Lamont, *Breakup: The Coming End of Canada and the Stakes for America* (Toronto: Key Porter Books, 1995).

Chapter 13:
Beyond Our Shared Continent: Canada in the World

For further reading on Canada in the world, the place to start is with the journal and publications of the Canadian International Council. See *www.canadianinternationalcouncil.org*. Also, visit the web site of the Canadian Defence and Foreign Affairs Institute for their very good publications at *www.cdfai.org*.

Each year McGill-Queen's University Press publishes the edited *Canada Among Nations* with chapters on different aspects of Canada's role in the world.

There are of course books that look specifically at Canada in the world, most often from left and right ideological perspectives. Notable examples are often from the nationalist-left, such as Linda McQuaig's *Holding the Bully's Coat, Canada and the U.S. Empire* (Toronto: Random House, 2007).

Chapter 14:
In the Groove: From Fear to Opportunity

John Holmes' *Life with Uncle: The Canadian-American Relationship* (Toronto: University of Toronto Press, 1981) is a fine and pithy treatment; his orientation and analysis are insightful and important.

Jeffery Simpson's *Star-Spangled Canadians, Canadians Living the American Dream* (Toronto: Harper Collins, 2000) is very readable and a good resource on population movements between the two countries.

John Ralston Saul is a leading voice in his concern for how a colonial mindset hinders our progress. Part three, titled "The Castrati," of his recent book, *A Fair Country: Telling Truths About Canada* (Toronto: Penguin Canada, 2008) is an excellent source for his analysis of this topic.

Hugh Segal's "North American Community, A Prospective to Excite and Inspire" (*Inroads*, Issue 13, Summer/Fall 2003) is striking in its call for a North American Community as a tonic for what he calls the "Canadian Disease."

Acknowledgements

I owe a number of "thank yous" from my professional and private lives to those who have contributed to this project's success.

Professionally, I want to thank James Iain Gow, my Ph.D. supervisor at the Université de Montréal. He is the master carpenter under whom I apprenticed.

While I met John Holmes only a few times, I owe a great debt to his book *Life with Uncle: The Canadian-American Relationship*, published in 1981. It made a huge impact on me as an undergraduate. When I started research for this book it was the first thing I turned to and it animated my first published article associated with this project – "Lessons from 'Life with Uncle.'"

In the writing and researching for this book, many helped me professionally by sharing, at various points, some of their time and expertise: Duncan Cameron, Anthony Wilson-Smith, Maya Mavjee, Lawrence Martin, Bob Rae, Dennis Stairs, Charlotte Gray, Earl Fry, Kim Richard Nossal, Robin Mathews, Andrew Cohen, John Ibbitson, Jeffrey Simpson, Paul Cellucci, Kerry Mitchell, Michael Kergin, Raymond Chrétien, Peter Donolo, Eddie Goldenberg, Colin Robertson, Roland Paris, Roy MacSkimming, John Pearce, and Anna Porter.

I'd like to thank the *Toronto Star* and Lee Berthiaume at *Embassy: Canada's Foreign Policy Newsweekly* for publishing opinion pieces I submitted throughout the project.

Also, thank you to the chase producers of CTV News Channel who "chased" me down, sometimes days, but more often only a couple of hours before "going live" — my website has a nice collection of those broadcast interviews. But more than that, while at times a distraction, it was great fun talking about Canada-U.S. relations on television. And to CBC Radio for getting me up at 5:30 in the morning to do up to thirteen different interviews at local stations as the sun rose across Canada.

I engaged this book upon leaving a job at Rideau Hall where I worked closely with John Ralston Saul and benefited from seeing firsthand the fierce commitment of a leading author to his work. As I set out on the project, Adrienne Clarkson helpfully talked to me about "forward momentum."

And then there are the people who worked with me directly on the project: Elise Kuurstra for some research and office support along with her sister Emily; David Nobbs for launching my web site; and Michael Benedict for his assistance with editing. As a former executive editor at *Maclean's* magazine, he helped me keep my thoughts concise and from straying into overly academic language. Also, thanks more recently to Andrew Chisholm who became essential for some research and in supporting my website *www.daviddyment.ca*.

And to other friends, who in unique ways, large and small, made a contribution, some shared a professional expertise: Henry Lotin, Glenda Fryer, Phil Goff, Piers Drew, Madeleine Drew, David Merner, Claude Schryer, Sabrina Mathews, Colin Challen, Stephen Baranyi, Lilly Nicholls, Marlow Purves, Jean-Pierre Cloutier, Nancy Strickland, Patrick Gibson, Barry Yates, Paul Dewar, Patricia MacDonald, Wendy Gifford, Antonia Maioni, Gar Knutson, Chris Sands, Stéphane Roussel, Monica Gattinger, Claire Turenne-Sjolander, David Biette, Gerald Wright, Roy Norton, Laura Macdonald, Bruce Campbell, and Gary Luton.

Friends and authors Eugene Lang and Stephen Dale, thank you for your encouragement and advice.

Friend and high school curriculum coordinator Gretta Bradley, thank you for writing the stimulating teacher's guide for *Doing the Continental*.

I want to thank Bob Rae for writing the foreword. I have always admired the important and progressive contribution of this leading Canadian to our national conversation.

Many thanks to my agent Robert Mackwood of the Seventh Avenue Literary Agency, with whom it has been a complete pleasure to work.

The talented and hard-working people at Dundurn are an inspiration: Kirk Howard, Michael Carroll, Beth Bruder, Margaret Bryant, Karen McMullin, and Jennifer McKnight.

I want also to acknowledge Carleton University and the Centre on North American Politics and Society where I'm currently senior research associate.

My students with whom I think about North American politics and Canadian foreign policy, to you the future in shaping this continent and our world.

My heartfelt thanks to my vibrant and kind parents, Mary and Douglas Dyment, who as always have been interested and supportive.

This project was a family undertaking, and four of us made the journey. To Oliver and Claire, our dear and wonderful children, and to Jane Gurr, my cherished life partner, I am deeply grateful.

Notes

Chapter 1:
Same Piece of Real Estate?

1. Raymond Chrétien, former Canadian ambassador to
   Washington, in an interview with the author on March
   30, 2009.
2. Lloyd Axworthy, *Navigating a New World, Canada's Global
   Future* (Toronto: Alfred A. Knopf Canada, 2003), 97.

Chapter 2:
Avro Arrow: The World's Fastest Fighter Jet Runs
Out of Fuel

1. The documentary *The Plain Truth* is described as "an
   investigation of the real story behind Canada's most
   famous aircraft that also explores the debate over its
   demise." In the documentary, one of Canada's leading and
   most celebrated historians, Professor Jack Granatstein, is
   interviewed at length. He is asked "Were the Americans
   the villains?" This is his answer: "To say the Americans
   killed it is, I think, simply not true. In fact, the Secretary
   of the Air Force in 1958 told the Canadian ambassador
   that if Canada wanted the Americans would buy the
   Arrows and give them to the RCAF. In other words:

to try to keep production going the Americans would actually give us some of our own aircraft. The Canadian ambassador, however, thought this was charity and said Canada had never accepted aid and this wouldn't fly."

The documentary can be found most readily as a special feature on the DVD of the 1997 made for TV CBC movie *The Arrow*.

Chapter 3:
Basic Steps

1. BBM Nielson Media Research.
2. Linda McQuaig, *Holding the Bully's Coat, Canada and the U.S. Empire* (Toronto: Random House, 2007).

Chapter 4:
Engaging a Preoccupied Partner

1. Jeffery Simpson, "Don't bite the hand that feeds you." *Globe and Mail*, May 7, 2004, A21.
2. Charles Gordon, "Hold that writ, Mr. Martin." *Ottawa Citizen*, May 1, 2004.
3. Allan Gotlieb, *The Washington Diaries, 1981–1989* (Toronto: McClelland & Stewart, 2006), 20. The first quote is Gotlieb, the second is Gotlieb quoting the British ambassador.
4. Interview with Michael Kergin, October 2, 2005.
5. John W. Holmes, *Life with Uncle: The Canadian-American Relationship* (Toronto: University of Toronto Press, 1981), 55.
6. Canadian School of Public Service, Action-Research

Roundtable on Managaing Canada-U.S. Relations, "Building Cross-Border Links: A Compendium of Canada-U.S. Government Collaboration," 2004, *www.myschool-monecole.gc.ca/research/publications/complete_list_e.html.*

Chapter 5:
Canada Is Not a Mouse!

1. Paul Sundell and Mathew Shane. "Canada: A Macroeconomic Study of the United States' Most Important Trade Partner." U.S.D.A., September 2006, 2.

Chapter 6:
Big Steps

1. North American Forum, "Continental Prosperity in the New Security Environment," Rapporteur Notes, September 12–14, 2006, Banff Springs Hotel, Alberta.
2. A good overview of these proposals can be found in: Danielle Goldfarb, "Beyond Labels: Comparing Proposals for Closer Canada-U.S. Economic Relations," C.D. Howe Institute, Paper No. 76, October 2003.
3. Teresa Healy, "Deep Integration in North America: Security and Prosperity for Whom?" Research Paper No. 42, Canadian Labour Congress, February 20, 2007, 16.
4. L. Ian MacDonald, *Policy Options* (October 2007), 3.
5. See data and supporting graphs at *research.stlouisfed.org/fred2.*
6. Thomas Courchene, "The Loonie and the FTA," *Policy Options,* October 2007, 55.

7. John Helliwell, *How Much Do National Borders Matter* (Washington, D.C.: Brookings Institution, 1998).

8. These figures are in U.S. dollars and are for 2006. For the U.S. generally: *www.bea.gov/newsreleases/national/ gdp/2007/pdf/gdp307p.pdf*; for the U.S. Great Lakes states *www.bea.gov/newsreleases/regional/gdp_state/2007/ xls/gsp0607.xls*; and, for China *devdata.worldbank.org/ AAG/chn_aag.pdf*.

9. North American Energy Working Group, SPP Energy Experts Group, "North America — The Energy Picture II," January 2006, 58.

Chapter 7:
Rules for the Dance

1. Janice Gross Stein and Eugene Lang, *The Unexpected War: Canada in Kandahar* (Toronto: Viking Canada, 2007), 328.

2. Canadian School of Public Service, Action-Research Roundtable on Managing Canada-U.S. Relations, "Advancing Canadian interests in the United States: a practical guide for Canadian public officials," 2004, *www.myschool-monecole.gc.ca/research/publications/ complete_list_e.html.*

3. "The Four Faces of Peace," Lester Pearson's Acceptance Speech of the Nobel Peace Prize, 1957, 7, *www.unac.org/ en/link_learn/canada/pearson/speechnobel.asp.*

4. Michael Byers, *Intent for Nation: What is Canada For?* (Vancouver: Douglas and McIntyre, 2007), 12.

Chapter 8:
What's Mexico Got to Do with It: Continental
Counterweight or Deadweight?

1. The sources of this data are: Senate of Canada, "Mexico: Canada's Other NAFTA Partner: Volume 3: Report of the Standing Senate Committee on Foreign Affairs," March 2004; and Mike Blanchfield, "Domestic scandal dogs visiting Fox," *Ottawa Citizen*, October 26, 2004, A6.

2. These quotes come respectively from two books published in 1984 one by Alan Riding and the other by Andrew Malcom.

3. Anthony DePalma, *Here: A Biography of the New American Continent* (Toronto: HarperCollins, 2002). Evidence of Canada and Mexico having a close relationship is thin: DePalma discusses two state visits between the two countries and a Canada-Mexico farm labour program.

4. Author's notes from a conference Northern Command, Ballistic Missile Defence, Homeland Security: Where Does Canada Fit?, A Conference on Canadian-American Security Relations, Institut d'études internationales de Montréal, 26 March 2004, Montreal, Delta Hotel; and Anthony DePalma, *Here: A Biography of the New American Continent* (Toronto: HarperCollins, 2002), 30.

5. Mexico in 2004 was the second largest supplier of crude oil to the U.S. after Canada and ahead of Saudi Arabia, exporting to the U.S. each day almost 1.6 million barrels. Source: *www.eia.doe.gov/neic/rankings/crudebycountry.htm*.

6. Lloyd Axworthy, *Navigation a New World, Canada's Global Future* (Toronto: Alfred A. Knopf Canada, 2003), 112, 122, and 124.

7. Anthony DePalma, *op. cit.*, 58.

Chapter 9:
An Energy Superpower Without an Energy Strategy

1. Peter Tertzakian, *A Thousand Barrels a Second: The Coming Oil Break Point and the Challenges Facing an Energy Dependent World* (New York: McGraw-Hill, 2006), 117; and Thomas L. Friedman, *The World is Flat, A Brief History of the 21st Century* (New York: Farrar Straus and Giroux, 2005), 407 and 411. Due to the sharp economic downturn production and consumption figures are of course forecast to drop significantly for 2009. Otherwise, the trends discussed in this chapter held for 2007 and 2008 according to a review in February 2009 of relevant statistics.

2. *Ibid.*, 3; and Hugh McCullum, "Fueling Fortress America, A Report on the Athabasca Tar Sands and U.S. Demands for Canada's Energy," Canadian Centre for Policy Alternatives, March 2006, page 21.

3. A speech by U.S. Senator (from Utah) Orrin Hatch "Hatch on Oil: World to Shift Focus to Unconventional Resources," delivered at the Canadian Embassy, Washington, October 17, 2005, 1.

4. Don Gillmor, "Shifting Sands," *The Walrus*, April 2005, page 35. The U.S. has less than 2 percent of the world's conventional oil reserves and no new refineries have been built in the U.S. for more than ten years; from: North American Energy Working Group Security and Prosperity Partnership Energy Picture Experts Group, "North America – The Energy Picture II," January 2006, 11 and Hugh McCullum, "Fueling Fortress America," 21.

5. From *www.eia.doe.gov/neic/rankings/crudebycountry.htm*; and Paul G. Bradely and G. Campbell Watkins, "Canada and the U.S.: A Seamless Energy Border?," C.D. Howe Institute, Commentary No. 178, The Border Papers,

April 2003, 3. One million six hundred thousand barrels a day from Canada is 15 percent of U.S. imports.

6   *Ibid.*, 3 and 9.

7. Barrie McKenna, "Addict's logic has oil-hooked U.S. in a fog about deficit realities, options," *Globe and Mail*, 29 November 2005, B16; and Pierre Alvarez, President Canadian Association of Petroleum Producers, "Energy," a paper prepared for the Canada and the New American Empire Conference, University of Victoria, November 2004, 2.

8. These sources of energy are: oil, natural gas, coal, electricity, and uranium. Twenty-seven percent of the uranium the U.S. uses in the production of nuclear power comes from Canada, this is the equivalent of over 5 percent of total U.S. supply of electricity, from *www.dfait-maeci.gc.ca* – *major issues, Canada-U.S. Energy Relations, Overview*.

9. These figures come from Pierre Alvarez, "Energy," 1; and from Jerome Davis, "North American oil and natural gas, current trends, future problems?", *International Journal*, Spring 2005, 429.

10. Monica Gattinger, "From Government to Governance in the Energy Sector: The States of the Canada-U.S. Energy Relationship," *The American Review of Canadian Studies*, Summer 2005, 328.

11. Though exports of oil to the U.S. have increased dramatically, Canada continues to import oil to meet 90 percent of demand in Atlantic Canada and Quebec and 40 percent of the demand in Ontario. In 2005 Canada imported, mostly from Venezuela, almost one million barrels a day.

12. These percentages are derived from data in Monica Gattinger, 328.

13. Admittedly, significant advances in 2009 and 2010 in gathering natural gas found in shale deep underground may be transforming our understanding of natural gas supplies and the future of this industry.

14. John Partridge, "Oil clouds sweet story of gas, by most measures gas plays bigger role in nation's economy," *Globe and Mail*, February 21, 2006, B19.

15. From *www.usembassycanada.gov*. All figures in this paragraph are for 2004.

16. Pierre Alvarez, "Energy," 1.

17. When American leaders call for "open and integrated energy markets rather than models that may hold patriotic appeal," they are speaking in the American national interest. And interestingly in this case with a touch of hypocrisy. From a statement by Karen Harbert, Assistant Secretary of the U.S. Department of Energy, "Western Hemisphere Energy Security", to the U.S. House Committee on International Relations' Western Hemisphere Subcommittee, March 2, 2006.

18. It is interesting to note that during the late 1950s and the 1960s the Canadian government had a policy of subsidizing Alberta oil through the National Oil Policy (NOP). Billions of dollars were spent to buy Alberta oil though imports from the Middle East were much less expensive.

19. The energy proportionality clause of the NAFTA (Article 605) says Canada must continue to export to the United States the same proportion of oil and gas as it has in the past three years, even if Canadians are running short. We can reduce exports to the U.S. only if we cut domestic supplies by a proportional amount.

20. Before the Free Trade Agreement with the U.S., the National Energy Board had a mandate to issue oil and

gas permits only if Canada had sufficient supply to meet its needs for twenty-five years.

Chapter 10:
Not Watertight

1. To give an idea of the scale of those exports, Turkey's deal with Israel to ship 50 billion litres a year is an amount equal to nine minutes of water flowing from Manitoba's rivers into Hudson Bay.
2. Ralph Pentland and Adèle Hurley, "Thirsty Neighbours: A Century of Canada-U.S. Transboundary Water Governance," 169, in Karen Bakker, editor, *Eau Canada: The Future of Canada's Water* (Vancouver: UBC Press, 2007).
3. John B. Sprague, "Great Wet North? Canada's Myth of Water Abundance," 25, in *Eau Canada*.
4. Richard Brennan, "Water Diversion, Great Lakes Deal, Premier Inks Pact on Lakes," *Toronto Star*, December 14, 2005, A18.
5. Michael Byers, "Don't water down Canada's deal," *Globe and Mail*, July 26, 2004, A13.
6. This is from the Council of Canadians, which as part of its campaign staged a twenty-city tour in 2008 calling for a National Water Policy.
7. Peter Lougheed, "A Thirsty Uncle Looks North," *Globe and Mail*, November 11, 2005, A15.
8. Study Group on Water Resources, National Capital Branch, The Canadian Institute of International Affairs, "The Transboundary Water Resources of Canada and the United States," 2005, 12, *www.ciia.org/nawgroup.htm*.

Chapter 11:
Defrosting Arctic Sovereignty

1. At 306 meters, the *Manhattan* was more than half as long as the CN Tower. The ship was built in 1962 and sent to the breaking yard in 1987. Humble Oil was the owner when it transited the Northwest Passage.

2. The passage of the *Manhattan* was a dramatic event for Canadians. As the leading scholar John Holmes writes "One reads now with blushes the excited debates in parliament when the *Manhattan* made its way into the Arctic seas. As editors and MPs saw it, it was rather like the Armada of Spain entering the English Channel." John Holmes, *Life with Uncle: The Canadian-American Relationship* (Toronto: University of Toronto Press, 1981), 115.

3. Some observers argue Canada already has the provisions it needs to regulate the Northwest Passage, as a result of the AWPPA combined with Article 234 of United Nations Convention on the Law of the Sea (UNCLOS) that gives Canada the right to control marine pollution from vessels and that anything else is nationalism. See: Suzanne Lalonde, "Arctic Waters: Cooperation or Conflict?," in *Canada's Arctic Interests and Responsibilities: Behind the Headlines*, 65, no. 4, Canadian International Council, 2008.

4. From my notes of Ambassador Thomas Nilles speaking at a Canadian Institute of International Affairs Conference in Ottawa on October 17, 1998.

5. A Northwest Passage clear of ice would be heavily used by commercial vessels as a much shorter route from Asia to Europe and the eastern U.S. While the ice is melting fast, navigation will continue to be difficult and the season short due to ice moved by currents and wind.

6. This understanding of the how Washington views this issue is largely from presentations, discussions, and interviews with speakers at the "The United States, Climate Change, and the Arctic" conference on April 19–20, 2007, in Montreal organized by l'Observatoire sur les États-Unis of the Université du Québec à Montréal.

7. Such a role for Canada is likely to be conditioned by a wider Arctic enforcement regime, which is beginning to emerge from meetings of a regional institution the Arctic Council, and would deal with such issues as Arctic pollution prevention and a polar navigation code.

8. Largely from "Appendix XVII, Legal Opinion on the Northwest Passage," by Donat Pharand, November 11, 2005, pages 215–33, in "An Interim Report of the Standing Senate Committee on National Security and Defence, Managing Turmoil: The need to upgrade Canadian foreign aid and military strength to deal with massive change," (October 2006).

9. A recent poll of Canadians found 44 percent felt Canada should unilaterally assert control of the Passage and that 67 percent felt that we can't trust the U.S. any more than the Russians when it comes to Canadian sovereignty. Views that will make it harder for Canada to pursue a compromise, as I am suggesting. The poll, *Canada and the U.S.: What Does it Mean to Be Good Neighbours*, was conducted by the Innovative Research Group for the Canadian Defence and Foreign Affairs Institute in 2008.

10. This notion of Canada protecting the U.S. through its responsibilities in the Arctic has some historical precedence. As relations in Europe began to deteriorate in the 1930s Prime Minister Mackenzie King told the Americans that Canada would ensure no hostile air bases were established in the Arctic.

Chapter 12:
Manifest Destiny and Quebec

1. Gordon T. Stewart, *The American Response to Canada Since 1776* (East Lansing: Michigan State University Press, 1992), 37.

2. J. L. Granatstein, "Free Trade Between Canada and the United States, The Issue That Will Not Go Away," in Denis Stairs, Gilbert Winham, ed., *The Politics of Canada's Economic Relationship with the United States*, (Queen's Printer, Alberta: Macdonald Royal Commission, 1985).

3. Charles F. Doran, "Will Canada Unravel?", *Foreign Affairs* 75, no. 5, (September/October 1996), 104.

4. Interview with Charles Doran, June 1, 1998, Ottawa.

5. The materials mentioned in this paragraph by Lamont, Lemco, and the U.S. State Department are: Lansing Lamont, *Breakup: The Coming End of Canada and the Stakes for America* (Toronto: Key Porter Books, 1995); Jonathan Lemco, *Turmoil in the Peaceable Kingdom: The Quebec Sovereignty Movement and Its Implications for Canada and the United States* (Toronto: University of Toronto Press, 1994); and Government of the United States, State Department, "The Quebec Situation: Outlook and Implications", August 1977, as published in: Jean-François Lisée, *In the Eye of the Eagle* (Toronto: HarperCollins, 1990).

6. Doran, "Will Canada Unravel?," 108.

7. Lemco, *Turmoil in the Peaceable Kingdom*, 152.

8. Lamont, *Breakup*, 224.

9. *Ibid.*, 231 and 233.

10. Lisée, *In the Eye of the Eagle*, 275.

11. Joseph Jockel, "If Canada Breaks Up: Implications For U.S. Policy," *Canadian American Public Policy*, September 1991, no. 7, 20.

12. Lisée, *In the Eye of the Eagle*, 300–01.
13. Doran, "Will Canada Unravel?," 98 and 109.
14. Jockel, "If Canada Breaks Up," 30.

Chapter 13:
Beyond Our Shared Continent: Canada in the World

1. Former U.S. President Bill Clinton in an interview with the author in Montreal on April 3, 2007.
2. To give a sense of Canada's size in the world, we are 33 million of about five billion people; about 1/150th of the world's population. In terms of our economy, our GDP is larger than India's and it was only in 2003 that China's GDP surpassed that of Canada.
3. Janice Gross Stein and Eugene Lang, *The Unexpected War: Canada in Kandahar* (Toronto: Viking Canada, 2007), 177.

Chapter 14:
In the Groove: From Fear to Opportunity

1. This understanding of the structure of values in North America is fairly widely held, see for example "Americans and Canadians: The North American Not-So-Odd Couple," a report from the Pew Research Centre in Washington, D.C., January 2004.
2. Jeffery Simpson, *Star-Spangled Canadians, Canadians Living the American Dream* (Toronto: Harper Collins, 2000), 17.
3. These figures are respectively from: *Star-Spangled Canadians*, 143; and, U.S. Department of Homeland Security, Office of Immigration Statistics, 2007 Yearbook of

Immigration Statistics, *www.dhs.gov.xlibrary/assets/statistics/ yearbook/2007/ois_2007_yearbook.pdf*, Table 32, page 84.

4. Hugh Segal, "North American Community, A Prospective to Excite and Inspire," *Inroads*, Issue 13, Summer/Fall 2003.

5. This point was made by Sidney Weintraub, a leading American advocate of further integration, in response to a question I asked him at a conference in April 2004.

6. John Holmes, *Life with Uncle: The Canadian-American Relationship* (Toronto: University of Toronto Press, 1981), 106.

7. Interview with Dan Akyroyd, a special feature on the DVD *The Arrow*, CBC Home Video, 1997.

8. Ken MacQueen, "Everybody Love U.S.," *Macleans*, December 3, 2007, 51.

9. Lawrence Martin, "North America's era of limitless integration draws to a welcome close," *Globe and Mail*, June 3, 2008, A17.

10. John Ralston Saul, *A Fair Country: Telling Truths About Canada* (Toronto: Penguin Canada, 2008), 114. Saul directly tackles the phenomenon in his aptly titled chapter "The Colonial Mind."

11. "Basic Facts About Canada-U.S. Trade," U.S. Embassy, Ottawa, January 2006.

12. Industry Canada Study referred to in Murray Dobbin, "NAFTA's legacy: the worst agreement we ever signed," *Globe and Mail*, Web Exclusive Comment, March 5, 2008.

13. "Deeper free trade," *Globe and Mail* editorial, February 4, 2009, A12.

14. Holmes, *Life with Uncle*, 2.

15. *Ibid.*, 111.

16. John F. Helliwell, professor emeritus of economics at the University of British Columbia, *How Much Do*

National Borders Matter? (Washington: The Brookings Institution, 1998).

17. Raymond Chrétien, former Canadian ambassador to Washington, in an interview with the author on March 30, 2009. The full quote can be found in Chapter 1.

18. Lloyd Axworthy, *Navigating a New World, Canada's Global Future* (Toronto: Alfred A. Knopf Canada, 2003), 97. The full quote can be found in Chapter 1. Axworthy is normally associated with the left-nationalist side of the debate.

19. The federalist Liberals have been in power in Quebec for three elections and the official opposition is the separatist Parti Quebecois.

20. Stephen Clarkson takes this view in his book *Uncle Sam and U.S., Globalization, Neoconservatism, and the Canadian State* (Toronto: University of Toronto Press, 2002).

21. Clayton Yeutter, who has a reputation for being outspoken, denies making this provocative comment. See: Bob Hepburn, "More signs the U.S. believes it beat Canada," *Toronto Star*, October 22, 1987, A25.

22. Holmes, *Life with Uncle*, 3.

Index

Acid Rain, 45
Afghanistan, 34, 42, 118,
    120–22, 128
Africa, 119
Airbus, 104
Alaska, 50, 96–97, 102, 107–08
    Boundary Dispute, 107–08
    Oil Pipeline, 96
    Panhandle, 102
    Purchase, 107
Alberta, 78–79, 82–83, 84,
    90, 91, 95, 109–10
    Oil, 79
    Tar Sands, 78, 80, 82,
    85–86
Ambassador Bridge, 48
American,
    Civil War, 108, 124
    Values, 17, 45–46, 66,
    118, 122, 123
Anthony, Nancy Hughes, 32
Anti-Americanism, 34
Apollo Project, 22
Arctic, 12, 34, 78, 80, 89,
    95–96, 128, 129

Islands, 97
    Sovereignty, 12, 18, 97–104
Arctic Cooperation
    Agreement, 99
Arctic Waters Pollution
    Prevention Act (AWPPA),
    98
Australia, 49–50
Avro, 19–25, 34, 86, 103–04,
    123, 126, 133
    Arrow, 19–25, 34, 86,
    103–04, 123, 126, 133
    Canuck, 19
    Jetliner, 19
Axworthy, Lloyd, 17–18, 74, 133
Aykroyd, Dan, 126, 139

Baffin Island, 97
Ball, George, 110
Ballistic Missile Defence
    (BMD), 12, 18, 34, 42, 64,
    67, 120–22, 128
Barlow, Maude, 33, 55
Baucus, Senator Max, 43
BBC World, 66

Beaufort Sea, 97–98
Biden, Joseph, 39
Bitumen, 85
Black Sea, 99
Bomarc Missiles, 21
Brimelow, Peter, 111
British, 105, 110
    Colonists, 105
    Empire, 107
    North America, 108, 124
British Columbia, 39, 50, 58,
    91, 102
British Commonwealth, 15
Buchanan, Pat, 111
Buffalo, New York, 50
Bush, George W., 36, 43, 45,
    53, 75, 104
Byers, Michael, 67, 142

Calais, Maine, 91
California, 39, 51, 72, 88, 92
Canadian-Mexican,
    Relations, 71–75
    Trade, 60
Canada-Mexico Commission,
    74
Canada-United States,
    Arctic Cooperation
    Agreement, 99
    Auto Pact, 108
    Border, 73, 91
    Boundary Waters Treaty,
    90

Free Trade Agreement,
    52, 57, 71, 134
    Reciprocity Agreement, 107
Canadian,
    Chamber of Commerce, 32
    Council of Chief
    Executives, 32, 54
    Defence and Foreign
    Affairs Institute, 158
    Embassy, Washington,
    D.C., 34, 37
    Identity, 16, 125, 128
    Left-Nationalists, 29, 60,
    96, 127
    Parliament, 41, 63
    Prime Minister, 40, 111
    Right-Continentalists, 29,
    38, 47–49, 52, 56, 127
    Canadian Broadcasting
    Corporation (CBC), 25, 30
Canadian Energy,
    Exports, 76, 79, 81, 84
    Production, 77
Canadian Labour Congress, 55
Canadian Trucking
    Association, 48
Capitol Hill, 11
Caribbean, 50
Cartier, George-Étienne, 124
Central America, 72
CF-18 Jet Fighter, 23
Cheney, Dick, 81
Chicago, 50, 90

China, 57–59, 66, 76–77, 85,
    120
  Energy Consumption,
    76–77, 85–86
  Rate of Growth, 85, 120
  Trade With, 66, 85–86, 120
Chrétien, Jean, 43, 45, 64,
    121–22
Chrétien, Raymond, 17–18,
    133
Churchill, Winston, 20
Climate Change, 92, 99
Clinton, Bill, 45, 117
Coal Bed Methane, 91
Colombo Development Plan,
    118
Colonial Mentality, 64, 123,
    126–30
Colorado River, 88, 89–90, 92
Columbia River, 92
Columbia River Treaty, 92
Concorde Passenger Jet, 22
Convention on Land Mines,
    118
Council of Canadians, 54
Courchene, Thomas, 57
Coutts, Alberta, 91
Customs Union, 33, 53, 54,
    61, 74, 125
Cyprus, 45, 87

d'Aquino, Thomas, 32–33,
    48, 55, 57

Darfur, Sudan, 117
Denmark, 97
DePalma, Anthony, 73
Desalination, 88
Detroit, 48
Devils Lake, 36, 91
Diefenbaker, John, 22, 120
Doran, Charles, 109, 112

Enbridge Inc., 85
European Union (EU), 47,
    66, 74

Florida, 49, 88, 124
Fox, Vicente, 53
France, 20, 30, 66, 112, 119,
    132
Free and Secure Trade
    Program (FAST), 53
Free Trade Agreements
    (FTAs), 61, 57, 59
Free Trade Area of the
    Americas (FTAA), 75
French Colonists, 105

Garrison Dam, 91
Gemini Project, 22
Germany, 30, 66
Glacier National Park, 91
Globe and Mail, 15, 19, 95, 131
Goff, Bruce, 15–16, 136
Goldenberg, Eddie, 64, 140
Gordon, Crawford, 21–22

Gotlieb, Allan, 37
Granatstein, Jack, 108
Grant, Ulysses, 107
Great Bear Lake, 96
Great Lakes, 58–59, 89–90, 92–93
  Fresh Water, 89–90, 92–93
  States, 59, 92
Great Lakes Binational Toxics Strategy, 92
Great Lakes Commission, 92
Great Lakes-St. Lawrence River Basin Water Resource Compact, 93
Great Lakes Water Quality Agreement, 92
Great Slave Lake, 96
Green Party of Canada, 55
Greenland, 97
Gretna, Manitoba, 91
Group of Seven, 16
Guatemala, 72
Gulf of Sidra, 99
Gulf Stream, 87

Haiti, 117, 118
Hans Island, 97
Harper, Stephen, 45, 59, 128, 140
Hart, Michael, 61
Harvard University, 16
Hayes, Rutherford, 107
Health Care, 30, 64

Helliwell, John F., 58
High Arctic, 97
High Plains Aquifer, 88
Holmes, John, 131–33, 135
Home Depot, 132
Howe, C.D., 21
Hudson Bay, 90, 91, 95
Hudson River, 36

Ignatieff, Michael, 57
Illinois, 59
Immigration, 17, 73
India, 57–58, 76
Indiana, 59
Indonesia, 99
International Criminal Court, 118
International Joint Commission (IJC), 38, 90–92, 101
Iran, 121
Iraq, 42, 67, 120–22, 128–29
Iron Curtain, 20
Irrigation, 88, 91, 96
Israel, 87

James Bay, 96
Japan, 48, 74, 76, 99, 127
Jockel, Joseph, 111–12
Johnson, Lyndon, 45

Kandahar, 64, 118
Kergin, Michael, 42, 44, 63

Kerry, John, 40
King, Mackenzie, 111, 158

Lake Michigan, 90
Lake Superior, 90, 93
Lamont, Lansing, 109-10
Lang, Eugene, 64-65, 121-22
Latin America, 72-73, 75
Laurier, Sir Wilfrid, 107
Lemco, Jonathan, 109
Libya, 99
Los Angeles, 124, 126
Lougheed, Peter, 37, 95
Louisiana, 22

Macdonald, John A., 98, 111
Mackenzie, Alexander, 132
Mackenzie River Delta, 78
Maine, 50, 91
Malaysia, 99
Manhattan Project, 16
Manhattan Supertanker, 98, 157
Manifest Destiny, 105-13,
    124, 128-29, 137
Manitoba, 36, 50, 91, 111
Manley, John, 37
Martin, Lawrence, 127
Martin, Paul, 37, 39, 45, 53,
    120-22, 128
May, Elizabeth, 55
McKinley, William, 102
McQuaig, Linda, 32
Mediterranean, 93

Mexico, 34, 38, 48, 52, 66,
    71-75, 93, 96, 124, 128,
    131
Farmers, 73
and NAFTA 52, 55, 60,
    71-75
Oil, 60, 73
Relations with Canada,
    71-75, 138
Relations with Latin
    America, 72
Relations with the United
    States, 71-75, 138
Trade with Canada, 71-
    75, 131
Trade with the United
    States, 59, 71-75, 127
Michigan, 49, 59
Middle East, 99, 121, 155
Milk River, 91
Minnesota, 50, 59, 123
Mississippi River, 36, 90, 91
Missouri River, 91
Monetary Union, 33
Monroe, James, 112
Monroe Doctrine, 108, 112
Montana, 43, 90, 91
Mulroney, Brian, 40, 52, 84
Multilateralism, 71, 74-75,
    118, 138

National Aviation and Space
    Agency (NASA), 22

National Energy Program
(NEP), 79, 82, 84
National Policy, 108
Natural Gas, 47, 51, 76-86,
94, 98, 128-31, 134, 138,
154, 155
Natural Resources Canada
FleetSmart Program, 56
Neche, North Dakota, 91
New Spain, 72
New York State, 50, 59
New York City, 50, 124
New York Times, 72
New Zealand, 15-16, 49
Labour Party, 15
Parliament, 16
Newfoundland, 93
North American Aerospace
Defense Command
(NORAD) Warning
Stations, 101, 121
North American Community,
54, 56, 66, 74, 124-25, 138
North American Competitive-
ness Council, 54
North American Energy
Working Group, 82
North American Free Trade
Agreement (NAFTA), 32,
39, 43, 52, 53-55, 57, 60,
65-66, 71, 73-75, 83-84,
86, 87, 93, 96, 105, 125,
130, 140

Dispute Settlement
Mechanism, 39, 43, 56, 59
Dispute Settlement Panel,
43, 120
NAFTA Plus, 32, 54, 57
Superhighway, 96
Temporary Work Visas, 125
North Atlantic Treaty
Organization (NATO), 21,
118, 119
North Dakota, 36, 91
North Korea, 121
Northwest Passage, 97-102,
138, 157

Obama, Barak, 11-12, 17, 45,
104, 134
Ohio, 59, 84
Oil, 37, 47, 60-61, 73, 76-83,
85-86, 87, 93-96, 98-99,
120, 128-31, 134, 138,
152, 154, 155
Ontario, 16, 19, 39, 49, 50,
82, 84, 90, 92, 109, 154
Organization for Economic
Cooperation and
Development (OECD),
29, 127
Oval Office, 11, 36, 43

Pacific Ocean, 90
Pakistan, 42
Parti Québécois, 111, 162

Peacekeeping, 119
Peacemaking, 119
Pearson, Lester, 45, 66
Pennsylvania, 59
PetroChina, 85
Plattsburgh, New York, 50
Point Roberts, Washington, 91
Polar ice, 19, 87, 99, 101
Polar Sea, 98–99
Progressive Activists, 55

Quebec, 16, 39, 53, 82, 92,
    105–13, 134–35, 154
    Quiet Revolution, 108
    Separatist Movement, 108

Radarsat-2, 103–04
Raleigh, Walter, 132
Realpolitik, 103
Recession, 131
Regan, Ronald, 40
Rest of Canada (ROC), 105–
    06, 108–10, 112
Rio Grande River, 89
Robertson, Colin, 34
Roosevelt, Theodore, 102, 107
Royal Canadian Air Force
    (RCAF), 21, 148
Royal Commission on the
    Economic Union and
    Development Prospects
    for Canada, 52
Russia, 78, 80, 97

Safire, William, 111
San Diego, 101
Saskatchewan, 89, 111
Saul, John Ralston, 127, 144
Scandinavia, 30
Seattle, 50
Second World War, 19, 21
Security and Prosperity
    Partnership (SPP) of
    North America, 38, 52–
    56, 57, 60, 65–66, 82, 153
    2005 Meeting in Waco,
    Texas, 53
    2006 Meeting in Cancun,
    Mexico, 53
    2007 Meeting in
    Montebello, Quebec, 53
September 12 Effect, 52
Simpson, Jeffery, 37
Skagway, Alaska, 50
Smart Border Accord, 53
Snowbirds, 49
Softwood Lumber, 43, 56, 59,
    83, 120
South Pacific, 49, 50
Southwestern Ontario, 16
Soviet Union, 21, 99
St. Lawrence Seaway, 101
St. Mary River, 91, 92
St. Stephen, New Brunswick, 91
Stein, Janice Gross, 64–65,
    121–22
Stewart, Gordon T., 107, 139

Strait of Malacca, 99
Sudan, 117–18
Suez Canal, 119
Suez Crisis, 119
Sweetgrass, Montana, 91

Tar Sands (*see also* Oil), 78, 80,
   82, 85–86, 141, 153
Teck Cominco Limited, 91
Texas, 53, 72, 88
The Arrow, CBC Movie, 25,
   139, 149
Third Option, 120
Trilateralism, 74
Trudeau, Pierre, 49, 52, 111,
   120
Turkey, 87
Twain, Mark, 58, 62

U.S. Environmental
   Protection Agency's
   SmartWay Transport
   Partnership, 56
U.S. National Association of
   Home Builders, 43
U.S.S.R. (*see* Soviet Union)
United Empire Loyalists, 105,
   124, 134
United Kingdom, 30, 42
United Nations, 87, 157
United Nations' Universal
   Declaration of Human
   Rights, 118

United States,
   Articles of Confederation,
   124
   Bureaucracy, 42
   Congress, 11, 34, 35–38,
   41–42, 44, 49, 55, 63
   Democrats, 134
   Dollar, 40
   Energy Imports, 79
   Federal Reserve Bank, 38
   Hispanic Population, 73, 75
   House of Representatives,
   35, 39, 43
   National Energy Policy,
   81, 84
   President, 41
   Secretary of the Air Force,
   21, 148
   Senate, 39, 108
   State Department, 109, 111
   Supreme Court, 92
   Undersecretary of State,
   110

Vancouver, British Columbia,
   91
Virginia, 101
Voodoo Jet Fighter, 23
Vulcan Bomber, 20

Washington State, 31
Washington, D.C., 34, 35, 37,
   39, 41, 63, 100

Watergate Hearings, 16
Weaponization of Space, 121
Weintraub, Sidney, 48, 161
Western Europe, 88
Windsor, Ontario, 48
Wisconsin, 59
World War II (*see* Second
    World War)
World Water Day, 87
Wright, Colonel Anne, 60

Yeutter, Clayton, 134, 162
Yukon, 50, 75

9/11, 45, 49, 52–54, 65, 124,
    135,

Of Related Interest

The War Room
Political Strategies for Business, NGOs, and Anyone Who Wants to Win
by Warren Kinsella
978-1-55002-746-4
$29.99, £14.99

Warren Kinsella's *The War Room* profiles and analyzes some of the best political warriors and spinners around. He employs personal anecdotes, political wisdom culled from his extensive experience on Liberal Party federal and provincial election campaigns, historical examples from other Canadian and American campaigns, and generous amounts of humour to deliver a book about what it takes to survive challenges not just in politics but in any kind of business or non-governmental agency, whether it sells music, movies, cars, or computers, or raises money to preserve the environment, combat cancer, or save animals.

Storms of Controversy
The Secret Avro Arrow Files Revealed
by Palmiro Campagna
978-1-55488-698-2
$26.99, £15.99

The development of the Avro Arrow was a remarkable Canadian achievement. Its mysterious cancellation in February 1959 prompted questions that have long gone unanswered. What role did the Central Intelligence Agency play in the scrapping of the project? Who in Canada's government was involved in that decision? What, if anything, did Canada get in return? Who ordered the blowtorching of all the prototypes? And did Arrow technology find its way into the American Stealth fighter/bomber program? Now, in this fully revised fourth edition, complete with two new appendices, the bestselling book brings readers up-to-date on the CF-105 Arrow, the most innovative, sophisticated aircraft the world had seen by the end of the 1950s.

Available at your favourite bookseller.

What did you think of this book?
Visit www.dundurn.com for reviews, videos, updates, and more!

www.ingramcontent.com/pod-product-compliance
Lightning Source LLC
Jackson TN
JSHW020020141224
75386JS00025B/617